THE
CROSS STITCHER'S
BIBLE
PROJECT BOOK

Jane Greenoff

D&C
David and Charles

To my husband Bill, whose love is everything,
and to Neal, whose advice and long friendship have made so many things possible.

Jane Greenoff, a self-confessed cross stitch addict, founder of the Cross Stitch Guild and designer for The Inglestone Collection, is one of the UK's most successful and popular cross stitch designers. She is the author of 17 books and spends much of her time teaching both in the UK and overseas. The Cross Stitch Guild's magazine *Stitch That* echoes her personal approach to stitching as does the CSG website (see below). Jane lives and teaches from her converted barn in Gloucestershire where she shares her life with her husband, two bearded collies and the occasional appearance of her two children!

A DAVID & CHARLES BOOK
Copyright © David & Charles Limited 2003, 2006

David & Charles is an F+W Publications Inc. company
4700 East Galbraith Road
Cincinnati, OH 45236

First published in the UK in 2003
First paperback edition 2006

Text and designs Copyright © Jane Greenoff 2003, 2006
Photography and layout Copyright © David & Charles 2003, 2006
Stitch Library artworks © David & Charles 2003, 2006 adapted from originals supplied by the Cross Stitch Guild

Jane Greenoff has asserted her right to be identified as author of this work in accordance with the Copyright, Designs and Patents Act, 1988.

A catalogue record for this book is available from the British Library.

ISBN-13:978-0-7153-1419-7 hardback
ISBN-10: 0-7153-1419-X hardback

ISBN-13:978-0-7153-2368-7 paperback
ISBN-10: 0-7153-2368-7 paperback

The designs in this book are copyright and are not to be stitched for re-sale.

Executive commissioning editor Cheryl Brown
Executive art editor Ali Myer
Project editor Linda Clements
Diagrams and chart preparation Ethan Danielson
Styled photography by Simon Whitmore; other photography by Karl Adamson

Printed in Great Britain by Butler & Tanner Ltd, Frome and London
for David & Charles
Brunel House   Newton Abbot   Devon

Visit our website at www.davidandcharles.co.uk

David & Charles books are available from all good bookshops; alternatively you can contact our Orderline on 0870 9908222 or write to us at FREEPOST EX2 110, D&C Direct, Newton Abbot, TQ12 4ZZ (no stamp required UK only); US customers call 800-289-0963 and Canadian customers call 800-840-5220.

THE CROSS STITCH GUILD

The Cross Stitch Guild was formed in March 1996 and quickly became a worldwide organization with an enthusiastic body of members – over 2,000 in the first six months of operation. As word spreads it is clear that cross stitch and counted thread addicts around the world are delighted to have a Guild of their own. The CSG has received an extraordinary level of support from designers, retailers, manufacturers and stitchers. Members receive a full-colour magazine that includes counted cross-stitch designs and technical advice. The CSG also supplies cross stitch kits, gold-plated needles, stitchers' gifts and Jane Greenoff's own classes. Its comprehensive website is open to all: www.thecrossstitchguild.com

For more information and a catalogue contact: CSG HQ, Yells Yard, Cirencester Road, Fairford, Gloucestershire, GL7 4BS, UK. Tel: from the UK 0800 328 9750; from overseas +44 1285 713799. If you have difficulty finding any products used in this book, contact the CSG who will supply by post.

Contents

Introduction

*A*fter the publication of *The Cross Stitcher's Bible* I was very gratified not only by the success of the book but by the very positive feedback I had from readers, many of whom were avid cross stitchers before but were now combining other counted techniques in their embroidery. As a result of the reception given to *The Cross Stitcher's Bible*, I was asked to follow it with a project book that echoed the themes, technical know-how and information, but also supplied lots of gorgeous, stitchable projects. I hope this is what you will find in the following pages.

This book begins with a useful section called Back to Basics, which includes information on materials and equipment you will need, how to use the charts and how to begin stitching. The book is then divided into four sections – Fabulous Fabrics, Exciting Embellishments, Perfect Stitches and Beautiful Bands. Each of these focuses on a theme, with projects that allow you to explore different fabrics, threads, stitches and types of embroidery. Useful technique panels in each chapter explain in words and diagrams the key techniques used in the projects. Apart from the main projects, which have full stepped instructions, I have included handmade cards and other creative items using small sections of the main charts. All of the stitches used are described and illustrated in the extensive Stitch Library and some of the stitches that were used in *The Cross Stitcher's Bible* are included here in an abbreviated form. Making up techniques, covered at the back of the book, show you how to finish and display your work beautifully. If you have any difficulties finding any of the embroidery supplies used in the book, telephone the Cross Stitch Guild.

All types of counted embroidery continue to fascinate me and I am sure I will never tire of seeing a design grow on a blank piece of fabric. If you are new to cross stitch, this is the beginning of a long association and if like me you are already an addict, I hope this book will inspire you to try even more counted techniques.

Jane Greenoff

USING THIS BOOK

The points here are general ones that apply to working the projects in this book.

● I have chosen colour charts with black or white symbols so that you can identify the colours you need but can still photocopy the charts to enlarge them for your own use.

● All the designs have been stitched in DMC stranded cotton (floss) unless stated otherwise. Anchor equivalents have been given where possible, though they are not always exact equivalents.

● Measurements are in metric with imperial alternatives in brackets – choose one or the other.

● Within each project you will find technical explanations and diagrams as necessary, featured in tinted technique panels.

● Refer to the Index for the various stitches used – they can be found in the Stitch Library with clear colour diagrams and explanatory text. The library also contains some stitches that were not included in *The Cross Stitcher's Bible*.

Back to Basics

This section refers to cross stitch and is here to remind you of some of the general information needed to stitch the projects in this book. It describes what basic materials and equipment you will need, how to use the charts, how to prepare fabric for work and how to start stitching. There are also plenty of tried-and-tested tips which you should find helpful.

Basic Equipment

Needles When working counted cross stitch you will need blunt tapestry needles of various sizes. A blunt needle is used because you should be parting the fabric threads rather than piercing the material. The commonest needle sizes used are 24 and 26 but the size depends on the project you are working on and personal preference. If you are not sure what size to use, check in the following way: when the needle is pushed through the fabric it should pass through without enlarging the hole, but also without falling through too easily. Avoid leaving a needle in the fabric unless it is gold plated or it may cause marks. A beading needle (or fine 'sharp'), which is much thinner, will be needed to attach beads.

Scissors Use sharp dressmaker's shears for cutting fabric and a small, sharp pair of pointed scissors for embroidery threads.

Frames and hoops These are not essential – I have worked without either for years, preferring to work cross stitch in my hand as this allows a sewing movement. If you prefer to work with a frame or hoop then choose one large enough to hold the complete design, to avoid marking the fabric and flattening your stitches.

Basic Materials

Fabrics The fabrics used for counted cross stitch, mainly Aidas and evenweaves, are woven with the same number of threads or blocks to 2.5cm (1in) in both directions. The warp and weft are woven evenly so that when a stitch is formed it appears as a square or part of a square. When choosing fabrics for counted cross stitch, the thread count is the method used by manufacturers to differentiate between the varieties: the higher the number or the more threads or stitches to 2.5cm (1in), the finer the fabric.

Tip

When beginning a project, check you have all the thread colours you need and make stitching easier by arranging them on an organizer card with their shade numbers. There are many commercial organizers available or you could easily make your own from stiff card.

Aida fabric is ideal for the beginner because the threads are woven in blocks rather than singly. It is available in many colours in 8, 11, 14, 16, 18 and 20 blocks to 2.5cm (1in), and in cotton, wool and damasks and as different width bands.

Evenweaves, made from linen, cotton, acrylic, viscose, modal and mixtures of all of these, are woven singly and are also available in different colours, counts and bands.

Threads The most commonly used thread for counted embroidery is stranded cotton (floss) but there are many other types now available. The projects in this book feature some of them, including metallic threads, space-dyed threads, silks and perlé cottons.

Beads Some of the projects feature beads, buttons, charms and other embellishments. There is a huge choice available so do experiment.

Preparing Fabric

Press embroidery fabric if necessary before you begin stitching and trim the selvage or any rough edges. Work from the middle of the fabric and the middle of the chart where possible to ensure your design is centred on the fabric. Find the middle of the fabric by folding it in four and pressing lightly. Work lines of tacking (basting) stitches following a fabric thread to mark the folds. When working with linen, prepare as above but also sew a narrow hem around all raw edges to preserve the edges for hemstitching when the project is complete.

Working from Charts

The designs in this book are worked from charts and are counted designs. The charts are easy to follow and are illustrated in colour with a black and/or white symbol to aid colour identification and allow you to photocopy them for your own use. Each square, both occupied and unoccupied, represents two threads of linen or one block of Aida, unless stated otherwise. Each occupied square equals one stitch. Some charts also have the addition of three-quarter cross stitches (sometimes called fractional stitches), French knots, beads and so on. These will be clearly labelled in the key beside the chart or on the chart.

When looking at a chart, try to plan your stitching direction. If you count across the shortest distances of empty fabric each time you will avoid counting mistakes. To prevent serious counting errors, rule a line on the chart to match the centre using a coloured pen.

You can turn your work and the chart upside-down if you prefer to work towards you, but never turn halfway – your stitches will end up facing the wrong way!

I make a copy of a chart so that I can lightly colour it in as I proceed to avoid looking at the wrong section. You may find a metal board with magnetic strips helpful as it keeps the chart in position and marks your place.

Calculating Design Size

Being able to calculate the eventual size of a design means that you will be able to decide how much fabric you need to stitch a project or whether a particular motif will fit a specific card, frame or other item.

All that determines the size of a cross stitch design is the number of stitches up and down, and the fabric thread count. Calculate design size as follows:

Count the number of stitches in each direction on the chart.

Divide each of these numbers by the number of stitches to 2.5cm (1in) on your fabric (the count).

For example, a design on 14-count Aida of 140 stitches x 140 stitches ÷ 14 = design size of 25cm x 25cm (10in x 10in).

If calculating design sizes for evenweave fabrics, divide the fabric count by 2 before you start (because evenweave is worked over two threads not one block as with Aida).

Always add a generous margin when calculating fabric requirements, to allow for stretching, framing or finishing. I add 13cm (5in) to both dimensions when stitching a picture or sampler. This can be reduced to 7.5cm (3in) for smaller projects. When creating a card or trinket pot, allow the margin on the aperture size, not the stitch count.

7

Starting and Finishing Stitching

Unless indicated otherwise, begin stitching in the middle of a design to ensure an adequate margin for making up. Start and finish your stitching neatly and avoid knots which create lumps. Two methods of starting are described here.

Knotless loop start This is a neat start that can be used with an *even* number of strands i.e., 2, 4 or 6. To stitch with two strands, begin with one strand twice the length you would normally need – about 80cm (30in). Double the thread and thread the needle with the two ends. Put the needle up through the fabric from the wrong side, where you intend to begin stitching, leaving the loop at the back of the work. Form a half cross stitch, put the needle back through the fabric and through the waiting loop. The stitch is now anchored and you may begin.

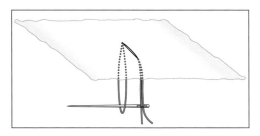

Tip

Increase the number of thread colours in your palette without buying more thread by tweeding. This means combining one or more thread colours in your needle at the same time and working as one to achieve a mottled effect.

Away waste knot start Start this way if using an *odd* number of strands or when tweeding threads (see Tip left). Thread your needle with the number of strands required and knot the end. Insert the needle into the right side of the fabric a little way away from where you wish to begin stitching. Work your stitching towards the knot and cut it off when the threads are anchored. The alternative is to snip off the knot, thread a needle and work under a few stitches to anchor.

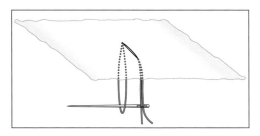

Finishing stitching To finish your stitching neatly, pass the needle and thread under several stitches of the same or similar colour at the back of the work and then snip off the loose end close to the stitching. You can begin a new colour in a similar way. (See also the stitch and park tip on page 18.)

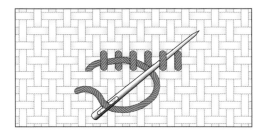

Cross Stitching on Aida

Aida is a fabric designed for counted embroidery and is woven in blocks rather than singly. When stitching on Aida, one block on the fabric corresponds to one square on a chart and generally cross stitch is worked over *one block*, as shown below. See technique panel on page 12 for more advice on working cross stitch on Aida.

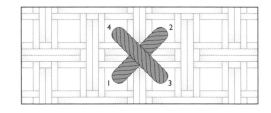

Cross Stitching on Evenweave

Evenweaves are woven singly and may be made of a variety of fibres. An evenweave fabric may have thick and thin fibres and even quite dramatic slubs in the material. To even out any oddities in the weave, cross stitch is usually worked over *two threads* of the fabric, as shown below. See technique panel on page 13 for more advice on working cross stitch on evenweave.

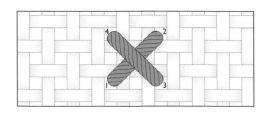

Stitch Perfect Tips

These tried and tested tips have been developed over twenty years of enthusiastic cross stitching and seem to cover most eventualities. I hope you find them helpful.

- Organize your threads before you start a project as this will help to avoid problems later. Always include the manufacturer's name and the shade number.

- Separate the strands on a skein of stranded cotton (floss) then take the number you need and realign them before threading your needle.

- Use the correct needle size for the fabric and the correct number of strands of thread: generally, the thread in your needle should be about the same weight as one of the fabric threads you are working on.

- If you must use a frame, try to avoid a hoop as it will stretch the fabric and leave a mark that may be difficult to remove. Moving a hoop across your beautifully formed stitches can spoil them.

- Start with the loop method when using two, four or six strands for a design. This method prevents the muddle so often found on the wrong side of a piece of embroidery.

- If tweeding threads (using one strand each of two or more colours to achieve a mottled, tweedy appearance) start with an away waste knot.

- Plan your route around the chart, counting over short distances to avoid mistakes.

- Work your cross stitch in two directions in a sewing movement – half cross stitch in one direction and then cover those original stitches with the second row. This forms single vertical lines on the back that are very neat and give somewhere to finish raw ends.

- Remember that for neat cross stitching the top stitches should all face the same direction.

- Avoid coming up through occupied holes (where a stitch has already been formed) from the back. Instead, insert the needle from the front. This prevents spoiling existing stitches.

- As you stitch you may find that the threads start to corkscrew slightly and spoil the stitches. Either turn the work upside-down and allow the needle to spin, or each time you take the needle out of the fabric give it a half turn before you re-insert it and the stitches will lie flat.

- If you are adding a backstitch outline, always add after the cross stitch has been completed to prevent the solid line being broken. Work the stitches over each block, resisting the temptation to use longer stitches as this will show!

- Try to avoid travelling across the back of the fabric for more than two stitches as trailing thread will show on the front of the work.

- When working with threads you are unfamiliar with, ensure that they are colourfast, particularly space-dyed threads. Press a clean, damp white tissue on to the threads and check that there is no trace of colour on the tissue. If so, do not wash the project.

Aida and Evenweave Roses

When I first starting stitching in 1984 the choice of fabric was simple – cream 14-count Aida or linen, bleached or unbleached! How things have changed! There is so much choice available now in embroidery fabric, both in thread count and colour, although the two main groups of fabric used remain evenweaves and Aidas (see Basic Materials page 6).

The fabrics in the Aida family are ideal for the beginner because they are woven with the threads grouped in bundles. This forms a square pattern on the fabric, which in turn creates obvious holes. See the technique panel on page 12 for cross stitching on Aida.

Evenweaves are woven singly rather than in blocks and may be made of a variety of fibres. Choice depends on factors such as your eyesight, the cost and the purpose of the finished piece. Working on evenweave isn't difficult, just different. Pure linen, made from flax, is often used for samplers, pulled thread embroidery and clothing but an easy-care fabric such as Jobelan may be preferred for table linen or baby linen. Refer to the technique panel on page 13 for cross stitching on evenweave.

The beautiful rose case shown here demonstrates how a variety of even-weaves and Aida fabrics can be blended in the same project. I have used parts of the chart to work a needlecase and a pin-cushion to match the case.

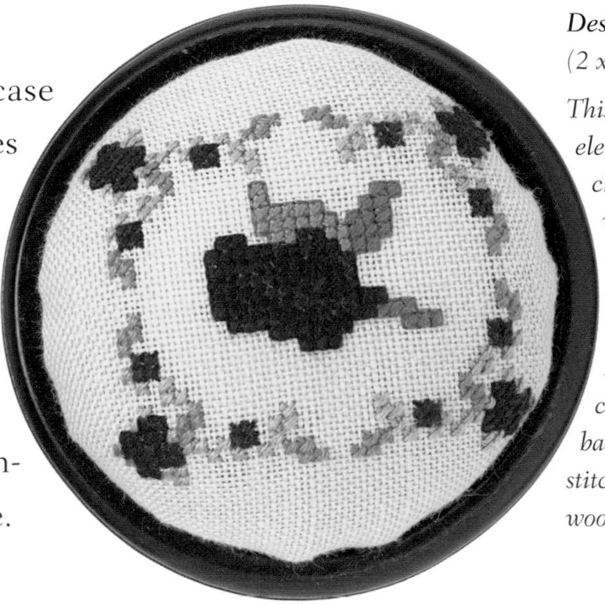

ROSE PINCUSHION

Stitch count 30 x 36
Design size 5 x 6cm
(2 x 2½in)

This little pincushion uses elements from the main chart on page 14 and was worked over two threads of Zweigart Cashel 28-count pale blue linen, using two strands of stranded cotton (floss) for cross stitch and one for backstitch. The completed stitching was mounted into a wooden pincushion base.

Rose Case

Stitch count

*161 x 101 (if worked
on one piece of fabric)*

Design size

*29 x 18.5cm
(11½ x 7¼in)*

YOU WILL NEED

*For front flap: either six pieces of 28-count
evenweave and 14-count Aida in various colours
or 41 x 30.5cm (16 x 12in) piece of 28-count
evenweave (or 14-count Aida)*

*For rest of case: 51 x 30.5cm (20 x 12in)
unbleached 14-count Aida*

Tapestry needle size 24

Stranded cottons (floss) as listed in chart key

*T*his is the perfect project for using up your spare pieces of Aida and evenweave. If you wish you could work the case on a single piece of material.
The front flap features six rose motifs, with a pair of rose-buds worked on the
lower section under the flap (see picture on previous page).

If working the flap on one piece of fabric:

1 Fold the fabric in four and mark the folds
with tacking (basting) stitches. Work the
front flap design, starting from the centre of the
chart and fabric. Use a loop start (page 8) and
work over two fabric threads for evenweave and
one Aida block. Use two strands of stranded
cotton (floss) for cross stitch and three-quarter
cross stitch and one strand for backstitch.

2 Fold the larger piece of fabric in half and,
with the fold at the bottom, work the rose-
bud at the bottom right of the top half using the
small chart on page 15.

Tip

All of the Rose Case
charted motifs could
be worked singly on
Aida fabrics and used
for cards, trinket pot
lids, coasters or
fridge magnets.

CROSS STITCHING ON AIDA

*Aida is a fabric designed for counted
embroidery and is available in 8, 11, 14,
16, 18 and 20 blocks to 2.5cm (1in) and
in many different colours and fabric types.*

● When stitching on Aida, one
block on the fabric corresponds
to one square on the chart, and
instead of counting threads as
with evenweave, you count and
work over single blocks.

● To work a
cross stitch on
Aida, bring
the needle up
from the wrong side of the fabric
at the bottom left of a block.
Cross one block diagonally and
insert the needle into the top right
corner. Come up at the bottom
right corner and cross to the top
left corner to complete the cross.
To work an adjacent stitch, bring
the needle up at the bottom right
corner of the first stitch and make
a cross stitch as before.

● Cross stitches on Aida can be
worked singly or in two journeys
– work half cross stitches along a
row and then complete the cross
stitches on the return journey.
Whichever way you choose, for
a neat effect, make sure that the
top stitches all face in the same
direction.

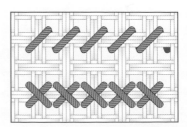

● Forming three-quarter stitches
on Aida is possible but is less
accurate than on evenweave
because there is no central hole
for the needle.

3 When stitching is complete, check for missed stitches, remove tacking (basting) and make up as a case with a bias binding edging (see pages 117 and 118).

If working a patchwork flap:
Work each rose motif on a separate piece of fabric, centring the design each time. When all six pieces are finished, make up as a case (see page 118).

> ## Tip
> Cross stitching in two journeys forms single vertical lines on the back which are very neat. This is particularly useful for table linen as you may be more critical than when the work is going to be framed.

ROSE NEEDLEBOOK

Stitch count 42 x 34
Design size 7.5 x 6cm (3 x 2½in)

This needlebook features the small rose-bud motif charted on page 15 and elements of the main chart. It was cross stitched over two threads of Zweigart Cashel 28-count pale blue linen, using two strands of stranded cotton (floss) for cross stitch and one for backstitch. A line of long-legged cross stitch (see page 110) was worked down the centre fold before adding a folded hem (see page 20). A piece of soft cream flannel was slipstitched to the inside of the case using the back of the long-legged cross stitch.

CROSS STITCHING ON EVENWEAVE

Evenweaves are available in a wide range of counts and colours. Because they are woven singly, threads can be withdrawn, making evenweaves suitable for withdrawn and pulled work – the gorgeous band samplers in this book show what can be achieved.

● To even out any oddities in the thickness of evenweave fibres, cross stitch is usually worked over *two threads* of the fabric in each direction, instead of over one block as with Aida. A 28-count evenweave thus has the same stitch count as 14-count Aida.

● Evenweave can be worked over one thread, for miniature work, for very fine detail and for text within a small sampler. When working over one thread, each cross stitch should be completed rather than worked in two journeys because part of the stitch will tend to slip under the fabric threads.

● When working on evenweave, start your first cross stitch to the left of a vertical thread. This makes it easier to spot counting mistakes because every stitch will start in the same position relevant to adjacent threads of the fabric.

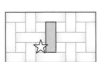

● Cross stitches on evenweave can be formed individually or in a sewing movement in two journeys – as described in the Aida technique panel, left. This quicker sewing method forms neat, single vertical lines on the back of the work and gives somewhere to finish raw ends neatly.

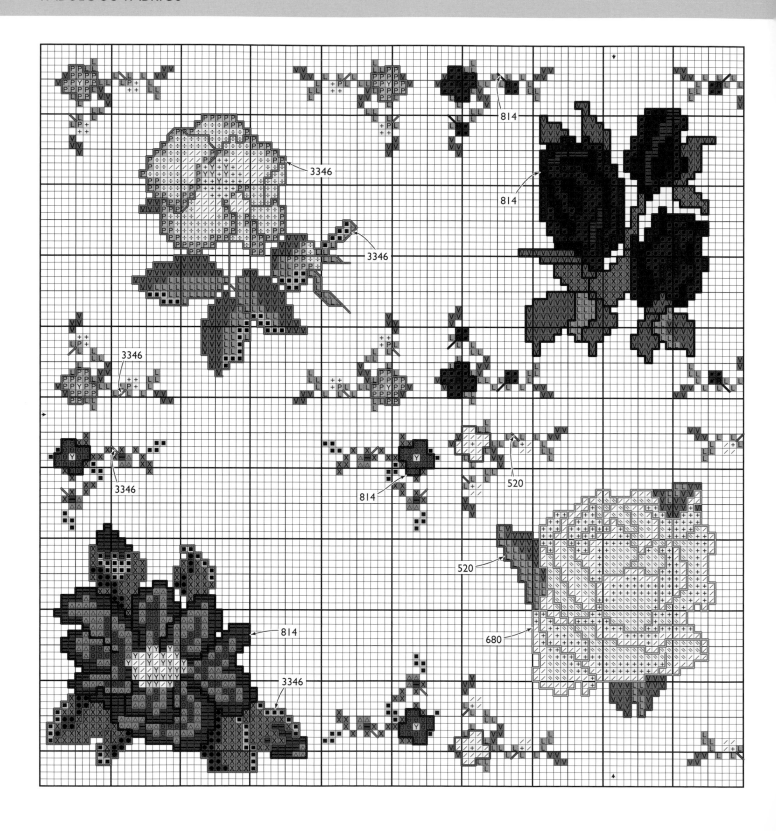

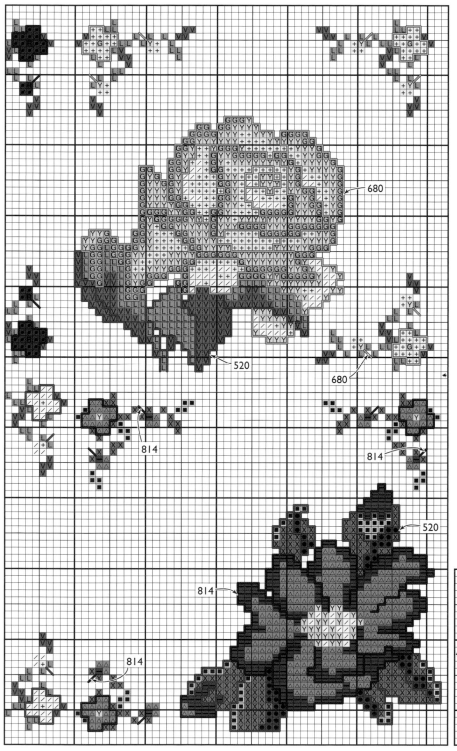

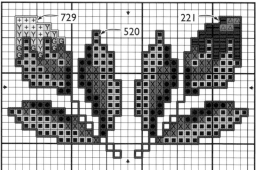

ROSE CASE KEY
Stranded cotton (floss)

	DMC	ANCHOR
	221	1006
	223	10
	304	47
	520	382
	666	46
YY	676	301
++	677	386
//	712	2
GG	729	306
	739	926
	814	44
PP	962	50
++	963	271
XX	3051	268
	3053	264
VV	3346	245
LL	3347	239
	3350	29

Elegant Evenweave

There are now literally hundreds of gorgeous fabrics for the counted cross stitcher, making it even harder to decide on any particular one. When selecting an evenweave material, think about the final end use as some fabrics will be more suitable than others. For example, baby linen and table linen need to be washable so choose something with an easy-care content like Jobelan. If you are looking for a crisper, feel, you may prefer pure linen or a linen mix. Try not to get confused by all the different fabric names and look for the colour you want.

Back to Basics described Aida and evenweave fabrics; the last chapter featured a project that patchworked Aida and evenweave together and provided tips for cross stitching on these fabrics. I have now added to your choices by suggesting the use of a patterned evenweave for this set of table linen! The projects here also show how a folded and hemstitched edge can finish off an item beautifully (see technique panel on page 20).

The Buttercup and Daisy tablecloth is a most unusual project as it has been stitched on a lovely checked evenweave fabric. Some of the motifs from the tablecloth chart have then been worked to create a co-ordinating placemat, napkin and coaster. All have folded hems except the coaster, which has a border of four-sided stitch and is then frayed. You could work all the designs on Aida if you prefer, although the pretty hemstitching wouldn't then be possible.

DAISY COASTER

Stitch count 40 x 40 (including four-sided stitch)

Design size 7.5 x 7.5cm (3 x 3in)

This charming coaster features Motif C from the chart on page 22 and was stitched over two threads of Zweigart Cashel 28-count evenweave, shade 633, using two strands of stranded cotton (floss) for cross stitch and one strand of 367 for backstitch. Work rows of four-sided stitch (see page 108) over four fabric threads using cream stranded cotton (floss). To create a frayed edge, count eight threads out from the four-sided stitch and pull out one thread on each side. Count out a further eight threads, cut away the excess and fray to the removed thread.

Buttercup and Daisy Tablecloth

*T*his tablecloth has a fresh quality, having been worked on checked evenweave fabric. It has a central panel, with two further motifs repeated around it (see picture, right). The stitch count is for the tablecloth as stitched but you could place the outer motifs in any pattern or position you wish.

Stitch count
292 x 292

Design size
53 x 53cm (21 x 21in)

YOU WILL NEED

140 x 140cm (55 x 55in) Zweigart checked 28-count evenweave (ref 7612 shade 56, CSG, Suppliers)

Tapestry needle size 24

Stranded cottons (floss) as listed in chart key

1 Fold the fabric in four and mark the folds with tacking (basting) stitches. Using a loop start (page 8), work the central design from the chart on pages 22 and 23 starting at the centre of the chart and the centre of the fabric. As the chart is a large one, you may find it helpful to photocopy the various parts of the chart and tape them together. Work over two fabric threads throughout, using two strands of stranded cotton (floss) for cross stitch and one strand for backstitch.

2 Once the central pattern has been stitched, work the outer motifs from the chart on page 21. I positioned mine like the points of a

compass, with the smaller motifs starting approximately thirteen squares out from the edges of the central design (see picture of complete tablecloth, right), but you could design your own pattern. If you wish to do this you may find it helpful to photocopy all the parts of the chart, cut them out and arrange them on a large sheet of graph paper, moving them around until you have created a design you like.

3 When all the stitching is complete, check for missed stitches, remove any tacking (basting) and then work a folded hem around the edges of the tablecloth, as described in the technique panel on page 20.

Tip

Use a 'stitch and park' technique when working with different shades, using several needles at a time to avoid stopping and starting. Work a few stitches in one shade and park the needle on the right side, above the stitching. Introduce another colour, work a few stitches and park again before bringing back the previous colour, working under the back of the stitches. Use a gold-plated needle to avoid marking the fabric.

DAISY NAPKIN

Stitch count 44 x 44

Design size 8 x 8cm (3 x 3in)

Stitch a pretty napkin using Motif B2 from the chart on page 21. Cut a 50cm square (19½in) piece of Zweigart 3240 28-count evenweave, shade 569. Measure in 5cm (2in) and remove one thread on each side in preparation for a folded hem. Count in sixteen threads from the missing one, work the cross stitch motif over two fabric threads, using two strands of stranded cotton (floss) for cross stitch and one for backstitch. The picture shows the napkin with threads withdrawn, before the folded hem has been worked – refer to the technique panel on page 20 for working the hem.

BUTTERCUP AND DAISY PLACEMAT

Stitch count 46 x 67

Design size 8.5 x 12cm (3¼ x 4¾in)

This placemat features a daisy from the main chart (Motif A1) and was stitched over two threads of Zweigart 3240 28-count evenweave, shade 205. Begin by measuring in 5cm (2in) and removing one thread on each side in preparation for the folded hem. Stitch the motif two threads in at the base and six threads in from the left. Use two strands of stranded cotton (floss) for cross stitch and one for backstitch. Work a folded hem to finish (see technique panel, right).

Tip

When working the coaster, remember that four-sided stitch is a pulled stitch so pull the threads quite firmly. The intention is to form holes to create a decorative pattern, as well as to prevent the fabric fraying.

SCORING AND STITCHING A FOLDED HEM

Many embroidery projects are beautifully finished off by a folded and stitched hem – not just the table linen shown here but also samplers (see Sea Breezes Band sampler on page 25). These instructions describe generally the method used for both table linen and samplers.

● From the middle of the long side (of a sampler) count five threads out from the edge of the stitching and cut the sixth thread. Carefully unweave this thread back to the corner and reweave it into the margin. Repeat this on all four sides.

● Lay the fabric *wrong side up* on a hard surface, count out from the missing thread to the ninth and tenth threads, place a tapestry needle between these threads and pull the fabric (not the needle) to form a creased line (shown in Fig 1 and in line 1 on Fig 2) – this will form the fold at the edge of the work. Repeat this on all four sides.

● Score the fabric again, nine threads further out (line 2 on Fig 2). Score another line seven threads out and cut the fabric following this line of threads carefully.

● Fold the fabric piece at the corners and cut as shown in Fig 3. Now fold in all the edges, mitring the corners.

● Hemstitch the folded edge in place, as shown in Fig 4, at the corners stitching the mitre with invisible stitching up the seam. I prefer to work without tacking so that I can see where I am hemming!

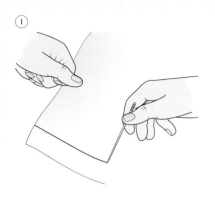

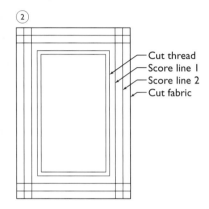

Cut thread
Score line 1
Score line 2
Cut fabric

Fold line
Cut line
Cut edge
Score line 1
Score line 2
Cut thread

Stitching

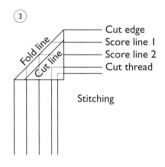

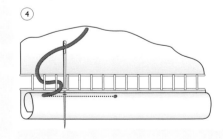

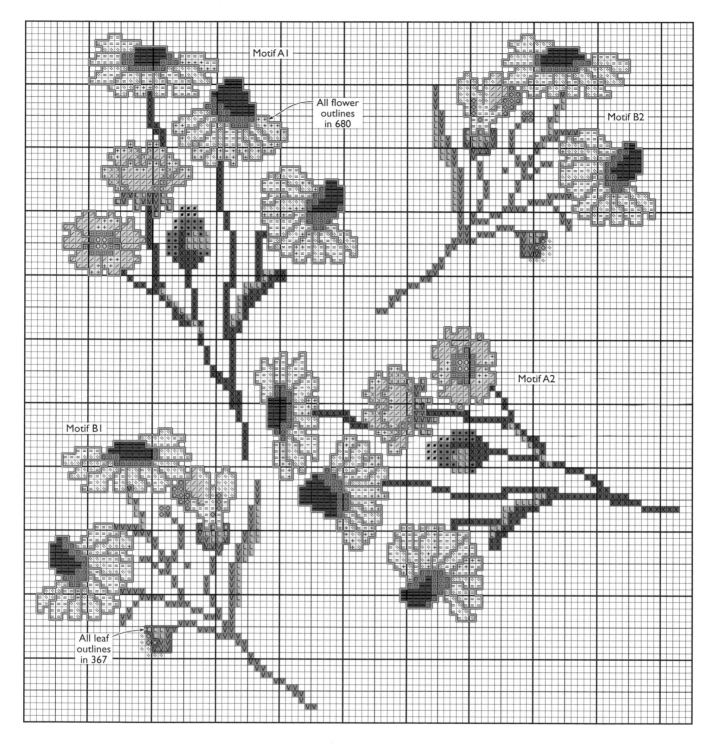

Motif A1
All flower outlines in 680
Motif B2
Motif A2
Motif B1
All leaf outlines in 367

BUTTERCUP AND DAISY (OUTER MOTIFS) KEY
Stranded cotton (floss)

	DMC	ANCHOR		DMC	ANCHOR		DMC	ANCHOR		DMC	ANCHOR		DMC	ANCHOR
	320	226		367	245		434	351		677	386		725	297
	351	33		368	213		503	240		680	307		729	306
	352	1094		402	311		676	301		712	2		blanc	1

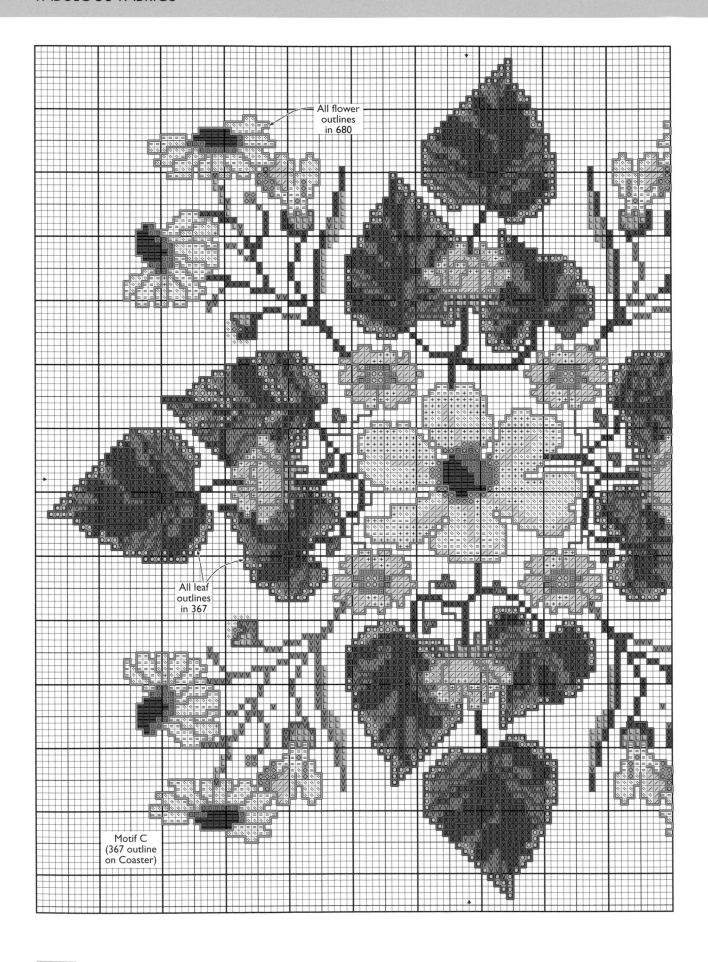

All flower
outlines
in 680

All leaf
outlines
in 367

Motif C
(367 outline
on Coaster)

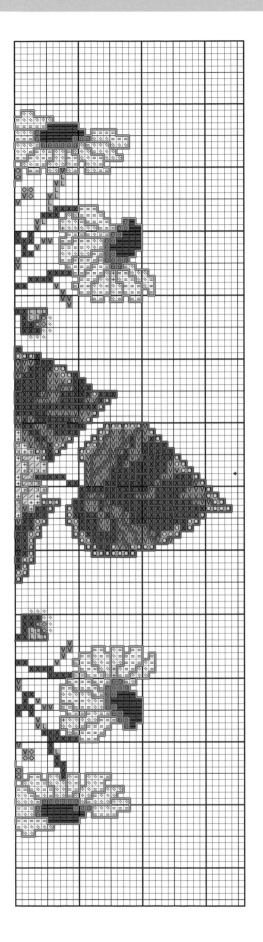

BUTTERCUP AND DAISY (CENTRAL PATTERN) KEY
Stranded cotton (floss)

	DMC	ANCHOR
	320	226
	351	33
	352	1094
	367	245
	368	213
	402	311
	434	351
	503	240
	676	301
	677	386
	680	307
	712	2
	725	297
	729	306
	blanc	1

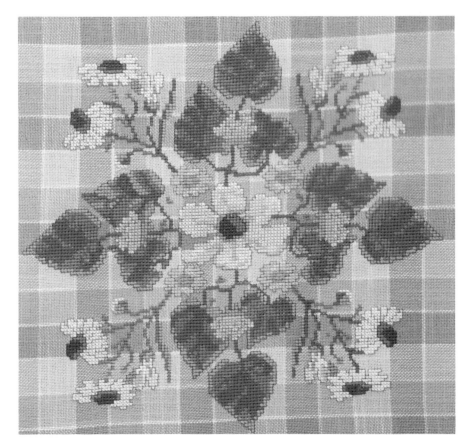

Linen Luxury

Linen is made from the fibres of the flax plant, *Linum usitatissimum* and has certainly stood the test of time: there is evidence in Switzerland of flax working as far back as 8,000BC, and linen cloths were found in the tombs of the Egyptian Pharaohs. When you start to stitch a special sampler you can be reassured that the fabric will outlive you!

Cashel linen, one of the dozens of evenweave fabrics available from Zweigart for counted embroidery, is a personal favourite. The choice of fabric colours is extensive, with many beautiful, subtle shades as well as lovely antique white and pure unbleached fabric. Some days, when I'm designing or doing office work, I almost have withdrawal symptoms and need to stitch on a lovely new piece of linen. It is so cool and smooth to the touch and handles so well.

The strength of linen makes it an ideal fabric for cross stitch, pulled or drawn thread work and Hardanger embroidery. Its characteristic creasing means that threads that are 'pulled' together stay pulled, creating lovely lacy effects. The projects that follow in this and later chapters illustrate the versatility of linen and demonstrate its qualities.

The lovely Sea Breezes band sampler (far right) illustrates the versatility of linen and includes hemstitch and Hardanger embroidery. Motifs from the charts are used to create a needlecase and are combined with a charming pram (baby walker) design to make the Beaded Birth sampler shown here. A gift card uses the pram motif again, to great effect.

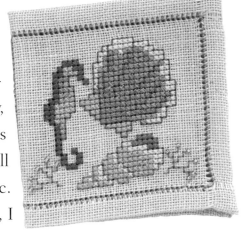

SEA BREEZES NEEDLECASE

Stitch count 30 x 34

Design size 5.5 x 6cm (2¼ x 2½in)

This pretty needlecase uses motifs from the band sampler chart on page 30. It was cross stitched over two threads of Zweigart Cashel 28-count linen, shade 224, using two strands of stranded cotton (floss) for cross stitch and one for backstitch. A line of long-legged cross stitch was worked down the centre fold before adding a folded hem (see page 20). A piece of cream soft flannel was slip-stitched to the inside of the case using the back of the long-legged cross stitch.

Sea Breezes Band Sampler

This band sampler, shown on page 25, is stitched in a combination of stranded cotton (floss) and multicoloured thread and would be an ideal first foray into the decorative stitches possible on linen. It has many pretty cross stitch motifs but also some more adventurous bands featuring different types of hemstitching and a small Hardanger motif.

Stitch count

45 x 153

Design size

8 x 28cm (3¼ x 11in)

YOU WILL NEED

21.5 x 40.5cm (8½ x 16in) 28-count Cashel linen, shade 224

Tapestry needles size 24 and 22

Beading needle or size 10 sharp

Stranded cottons (floss) as listed in chart key

Anchor Multicolour stranded cotton (floss) 1345

Perlé cotton No 8 ecru

Perlé cotton No 12 ecru

Mill Hill glass seed beads, pearl (00123) and pale blue (00143)

1 It is important to prepare the linen for work and mark guidelines, see page 7. Start stitching in the middle of the fabric and from the centre of the chart to ensure adequate space for finishing. Follow the chart on pages 30 and 31. Work the design over two fabric threads, completing the zigzag part of Band 6 first to help to 'get your eye in' before attempting any of the other decorative stitches.

2 Work a line of tacking (basting) stitches down each side of the fabric starting at the end of the completed cross stitch band. This will help to place the next stitches and act as a warning if you have miscounted. All the bands are worked in cross stitch except those detailed below. Page numbers refer to diagrams or detailed instructions for some stitches.

Use two strands of stranded cotton (floss) for full and three-quarter cross stitches, eyelets, satin stitch, bullion stitch, French knots, half Rhodes stitch and long stitch. Work backstitch outlines and Holbein (double running stitch) in one strand. Work Kloster blocks in one strand of ecru perlé cotton No 8. Work the needleweaving and hemstitch bands with one strand of ecru perlé cotton No 12. Add woven leaves, woven fans and the crossed lines in the centre of the Hardanger in Anchor Multicolour stranded cotton 1345 using two strands.

Use a beading needle to attach beads, with one strand of cream thread and a half cross stitch (see technique panel on page 43).

3 When the band sampler is complete, either hemstitch the edges as described on page 20 or mount and frame as a picture (see page 116 for advice).

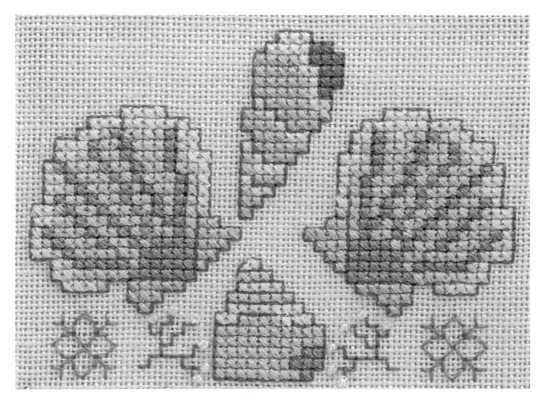

BANDS 1, 2, 4, 5, 8, 11, 12, 14 & 15
Assorted motifs in cross stitch, Holbein stitch, eyelets, long stitch and beads
See technique panel page 67 for working Holbein stitch and page 55 for working eyelets.

BANDS 3, 7, 10 & 13 Hemstitch, tied hemstitch, ladder hemstitch and herringbone
To work the hemstitch bands refer to technique panel on page 28. Following the instructions on the chart, hemstitch the remaining verticals using the strands and colours on the chart.

BAND 6 Cross stitch, satin stitch and Hardanger motif
Use one strand of ecru perlé cotton No 8 to work Kloster blocks and one strand perlé No 12

for the needleweaving (see technique panels on pages 74 and 77). See also the small chart page 79 as an example of which threads may be cut. Work woven leaf and woven fan filling stitches (see page 113) in two strands of multicolour 1345. Work the large cross in the centre of the Hardanger motif in 1345, twisting the thread.

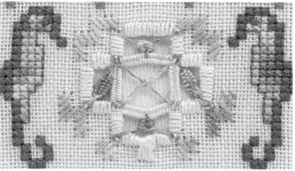

BAND 9 Bullion stitches, French knots, beads
Outline the row in backstitch as charted. Add random bullion stitches and French knots in blues and multicolour, and pearl and blue beads.

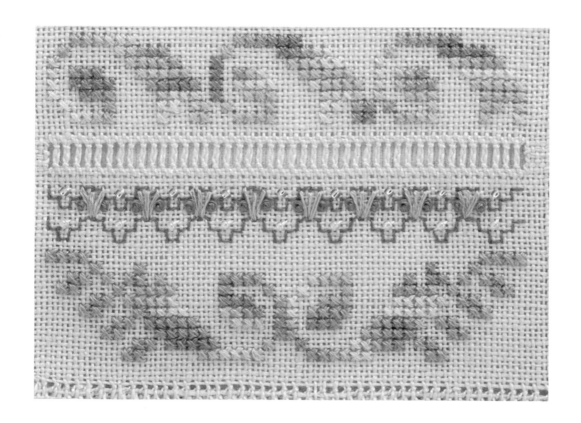

Beaded Birth Sampler

*T*his delicate little birth sampler, shown on page 25, has been designed to suit either a girl or boy so you don't need to await the arrival before beginning to stitch! Initials and dates can be added in backstitch.

Stitch count	Design size
44 x 68	8 x 12.5cm (3 x 5in)

YOU WILL NEED

20 x 25.5cm (8 x 10in) Zweigart Cashel 28-count linen, shade 224

Tapestry needle size 24

Beading needle or size 10 sharp

Stranded cottons (floss) as listed in chart key

Mill Hill glass seed beads, pale blue (00143) and pale pink (00145)

1 Fold the fabric in four and mark the folds with tacking (basting) stitches. Work the design from the centre of the chart and fabric. Work the various stitches over two fabric threads, using a loop start (see page 8) and two strands of stranded cotton (floss) for cross stitch, eyelets, Rhodes stitch and half Rhodes, and one strand for backstitch and Holbein stitch.

2 To work Band 2, outline the row in backstitch as shown on the chart. Then, working at random, add the bullion stitches and French knots in the colours used in the sampler, adding beads at will. Use a beading needle to add the beads after the cross stitch is complete using matching thread and a half cross stitch.

3 When the stitching is complete, check for missed stitches, remove any tacking (basting) and make up into a picture with a double mount (see page 116).

WORKING HEMSTITCH

Hemstitch is wonderfully versatile, allowing you to hem raw edges, form folded hems (see page 20) or remove horizontal threads and decorate the verticals in many ways. (See Stitch Library page 114.)

● To remove horizontal threads prior to hemstitching, count carefully to the centre of the band and cut horizontal threads (refer to chart for how many threads). Using a needle, un-pick the linen threads back to the edge of the band (see chart for how many). Working in pairs, remove one thread completely and reweave the other into the gap (see ladder hemstitch diagram below). Continue until all the threads are removed or rewoven.

BASIC HEMSTITCH

Turn the work so that the band is at right angles and you are working down the band. Work a straight stitch across two threads horizontally, turning the needle vertically. Now pick up two of the newly formed threads, make another straight stitch across two threads at right angles to the first stitch, then pass the needle down diagonally under the two threads. Repeat the straight stitches along the row, counting carefully.

LADDER HEMSTITCH

Having removed the fabric threads, work two rows of hemstitch as described above. The remaining vertical threads form a ladder pattern.

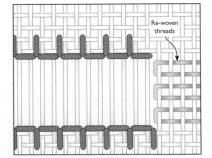

Re-woven threads

TIED HEMSTITCH

Begin by stitching two rows of hemstitch as above. Take the needle and thread over a group of four threads (or as on the chart), knotting them round. Ensure the tying thread is straight.

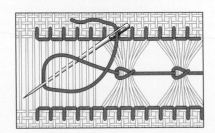

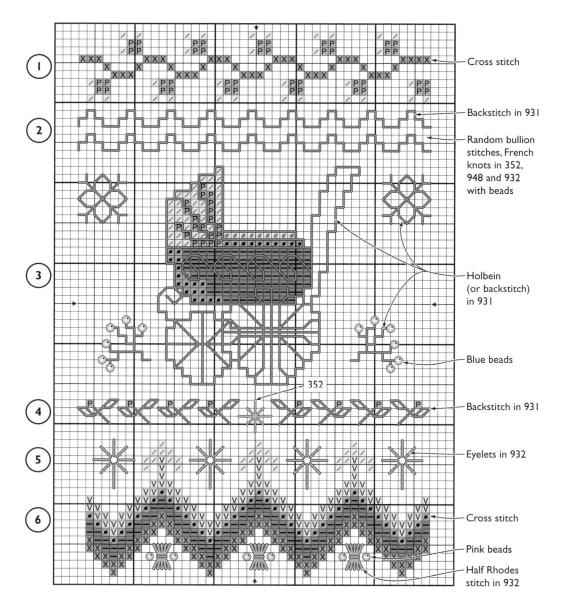

BEADED BIRTH SAMPLER KEY

Stranded cotton (floss)

	DMC	ANCHOR
P P / P P	352	1094
/ / / /	754	271
+ + / + +	809	1062
▨ ▨ / ▨ ▨	842	387
X X / X X	926	208
▬ ▬	931	978
▨ ▨ / ▨ ▨	932	129
▨ ▨ / ▨ ▨	948	271
V V / V V	3752	1037

Mill Hill Glass Beads

- 00143 pale blue
- 00145 pale pink

Labels on chart:
- Cross stitch
- Backstitch in 931
- Random bullion stitches, French knots in 352, 948 and 932 with beads
- Holbein (or backstitch) in 931
- Blue beads
- 352
- Backstitch in 931
- Eyelets in 932
- Cross stitch
- Pink beads
- Half Rhodes stitch in 932

NEW BABY GIFT CARD

Stitch count 25 x 27

Design size 4.5 x 5cm (1¾ x 2in)

This gorgeous little card features the pram motif from the Beaded Birth sampler on 14-count white Aida, using two strands of stranded cotton (floss) for cross stitch and one for backstitch. The fabric was trimmed, frayed and mounted with double-sided adhesive tape on to white card decorated with pink dolls' house wallpaper.

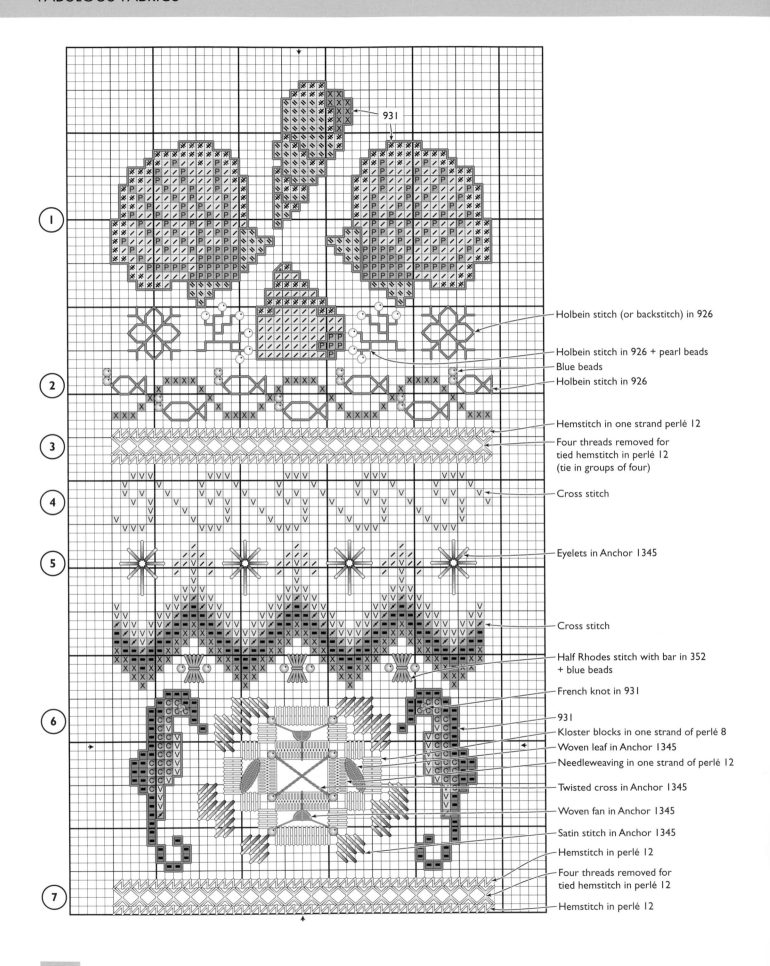

931

Holbein stitch (or backstitch) in 926

Holbein stitch in 926 + pearl beads
Blue beads
Holbein stitch in 926

Hemstitch in one strand perlé 12
Four threads removed for
tied hemstitch in perlé 12
(tie in groups of four)

Cross stitch

Eyelets in Anchor 1345

Cross stitch

Half Rhodes stitch with bar in 352
+ blue beads

French knot in 931

931
Kloster blocks in one strand of perlé 8
Woven leaf in Anchor 1345
Needleweaving in one strand of perlé 12

Twisted cross in Anchor 1345

Woven fan in Anchor 1345

Satin stitch in Anchor 1345

Hemstitch in perlé 12

Four threads removed for
tied hemstitch in perlé 12

Hemstitch in perlé 12

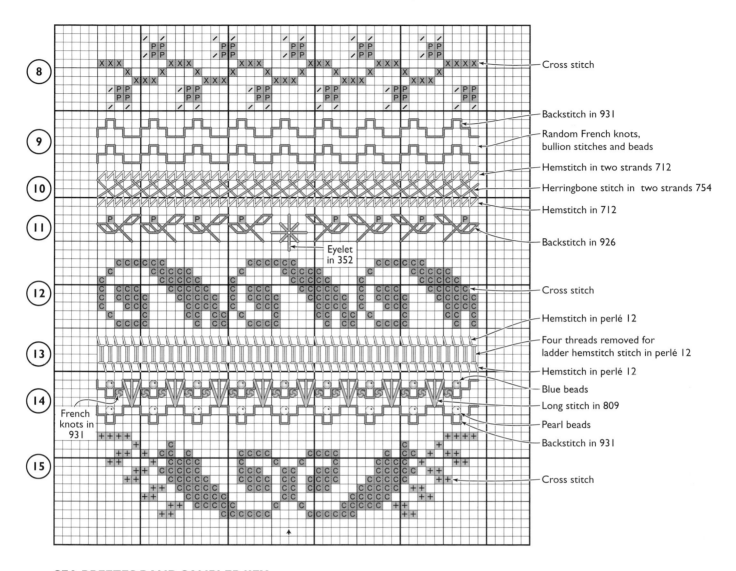

The following labels appear to the right of the chart:

- Cross stitch
- Backstitch in 931
- Random French knots, bullion stitches and beads
- Hemstitch in two strands 712
- Herringbone stitch in two strands 754
- Hemstitch in 712
- Backstitch in 926
- Eyelet in 352
- Cross stitch
- Hemstitch in perlé 12
- Four threads removed for ladder hemstitch stitch in perlé 12
- Hemstitch in perlé 12
- Blue beads
- Long stitch in 809
- Pearl beads
- Backstitch in 931
- Cross stitch

Labels on the left:

- French knots in 931

Row numbers: 8, 9, 10, 11, 12, 13, 14, 15

SEA BREEZES BAND SAMPLER KEY

Stranded cotton (floss)

	DMC	ANCHOR		DMC	ANCHOR	Mill Hill Glass Beads	
PP/PP	352	1094	▪▪/▪▪	931	978		00123 pearl
GG/GG	415	847	////	932	129		00143 pale blue
////	754	271	✳✳/✳✳	948	271		
++/++	809	1062	VV/VV	3752	1037		
✺✺/✺✺	842	387	CC/CC	Anchor Multicolour 1345			
XX/XX	926	208	▬	Anchor Multicolour 1345			

Glorious Threads

I would need to write a complete book to include all the marvellous threads and fibres available to the stitcher today, so I have devoted this section to just metallics and blending filaments. Working with these threads can sometimes be a little trying as they can have a mind of their own, but in this section I give tips and hints to make the whole process trouble free.

Many companies now produce metallic threads but Au Ver à Soie was the first company to produce blending filaments, with a particularly lovely pearl lustre that I love. I have also used Coats Ophir thread, a viscose/polyester mixture which gives the appearance of metallic thread.

A glitzy, grown-up advent calendar is featured in this chapter. It's a perfect project for showing off metallic threads and is designed to take a liqueur chocolate in each pocket – a chance for the adults to have a treat whilst preparing for Christmas. The designs on each pocket have been stitched using stranded cottons (floss) combined with various sparkly metallic threads and blending filaments to create a really sumptuous effect. Full making up instructions are provided on page 117.

I have taken six of the motifs from this main design, working them on small pieces of Aida to create Christmas cards, tree decorations and cracker trims using festive ribbons, wrapping paper and card. As you can see the only limit here is your imagination! For card making instructions see page 118.

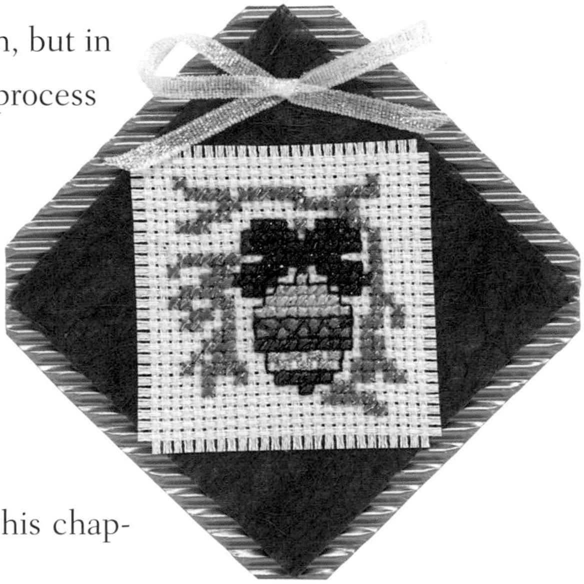

**TREE BAUBLE
GIFT CARD**

Stitch count 22 x 22

*Design size 4 x 4cm
(1½ x 1½in)*

This motif from the main chart was stitched on 14-count Zweigart cream Aida, using two strands of stranded cotton (floss) combined with sparkly threads for cross stitch and one strand for backstitch. The stitching was trimmed, frayed and attached to a piece of silk paper and corrugated gold card using double-sided adhesive tape and trimmed with festive ribbon.

Sparkly Advent Calendar

*T*his attractive calendar is simple to stitch, the addition of metallic threads making it into something quite special. There are twenty-four Christmas motifs, four stitched on each of six 40.5cm (16in) lengths of linen band. My version is worked on linen band but a 14-count Aida band could also be used.

ORANGE AND CLOVE TREE TRIM

Stitch count *19 x 20*

Design size *3.5 x 3.75cm (1⅜ x 1½in)*

This design from the main chart was stitched on 14-count Zweigart Yorkshire Aida, using two strands of stranded cotton (floss) combined with sparkly threads for cross stitch and one strand for backstitch. Random French knots were added using two strands. The back of the stitching was painted with PVA glue, dried and cut out. The stitching was stuck to a small roll of music wrapping paper and tied with festive ribbon.

Stitch count
22 x 22 (each pocket)

Design size
4 x 4cm (1½ x 1½in)
(each pocket)

YOU WILL NEED

2.5m (100in) length of 28-count ivory linen band (ref 980/60 see CSG, Suppliers)

Tapestry needle size 24

Beading needle or size 10 sharp

Stranded cotton (floss) as listed in chart key

Kreinik blending filaments as in chart key

Au Ver à Soie 003

Anchor Ophir 300

Mill Hill Petite glass beads, lustre (42010)

Assorted festive ribbons (see Suppliers)

Pineapple bell pull ends (see CSG, Suppliers)

1 Cut the linen band into six 40.5cm (16in) lengths and work narrow hems along the ends to prevent fraying.

2 To ensure that the motifs are positioned correctly, mark the band with tacking (basting) lines – each pocket is twenty-two stitches square with ten stitches (twenty threads or ten blocks if working on Aida) between each motif.

3 Work each design in the centre of the marked squares over two fabric threads (or over one block of Aida), following the chart on pages 36–39. Use two strands of stranded cotton (floss) for cross stitch and one for backstitch. Where the stranded cotton (floss) is combined with other threads, thread the needle with the metallic or blending filament, knotting as shown in the technique panel opposite, adding the stranded cotton (floss) afterwards.

4 Work the French knots and Algerian eyes after the cross stitch is complete using two strands of stranded cotton (floss) in the shades indicated on the chart. Use a beading needle to attach the beads, with one strand of matching thread and a half cross stitch.

5 When the stitching is complete, remove any tacking (basting) and refer to page 117 for making up and for making bias binding.

CHRISTMAS PUDDING CARD

Stitch count *21 x 21*

Design size *4 x 4cm (1½ x 1½in)*

This jolly motif was stitched on 14-count Zweigart gold-flecked Aida using two strands of stranded cotton (floss) combined with sparkly threads for cross stitch and one strand for backstitch. The stitching was attached to red corrugated card and trimmed with tartan and gold ribbon.

CHRISTMAS TREE CARD

Stitch count 18 x 22

Design size 3.25 x 4cm (1¼ x 1½in)

This design was stitched on 14-count Zweigart silver-flecked Aida using two strands of stranded cotton (floss) combined with sparkly threads for cross stitch and one strand for backstitch. The stitching was frayed and attached with double-sided tape to a handmade card of gold wrapping paper, ribbons and torn silk paper.

FIREPLACE AND PRESENTS CARD

Stitch count 21 x 21

Design size 4 x 4cm (1½ x 1½in)

This cheerful scene from the main chart was stitched on 14-count Zweigart gold-flecked Aida using two strands of stranded cotton (floss) combined with sparkly threads for cross stitch and one strand for backstitch. The stitching was frayed, attached to red card and trimmed with gold ribbon.

CHRISTMAS STOCKING TREE TRIM

Stitch count 19 x 20

Design size 3.5 x 3.75cm (1⅜ x 1½in)

This motif was stitched on 16-count Zweigart cream Aida using two strands of stranded cotton (floss) combined with sparkly threads for cross stitch and one strand for backstitch. The stitching was frayed and attached to red card cut with fancy-edged scissors and a gold ribbon loop added.

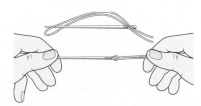

WORKING WITH METALLIC THREADS AND BLENDING FILAMENTS

Metallic threads and blending filaments can create some wonderful effects, especially with so many colours and textures available nowadays. You can vary the amount of shine by increasing or decreasing the number of strands used.

● Stitch slowly and attentively and use the 'stab' method rather than the 'hand sewing' method, working stitches in two movements – up vertically, then down vertically through the fabric. Let your needle hang after every few stitches to allow the thread to untwist.

● Use short lengths of thread, 46cm (18in), to avoid excessive abrasion when pulling through the fabric.

● Use a needle large enough to open a hole in the fabric sufficiently to allow the thread to go through easily.

● To thread metallic threads and blending filaments, fold the thread about 5cm (2in) from one end and insert the loop through the eye of the needle leaving a short tail. Pull the loop over the needle's point and tighten at the end of the eye to secure. Stroke the knot thread to secure in place.

● To thread metallic braids and ribbons, place a small strip of folded paper through the eye of the needle, open out the ends and insert the thread between them. Gently pull the paper through so the thread is brought with it.

Row 1

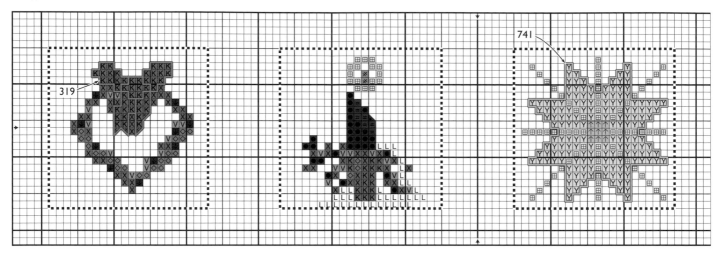

Row 2

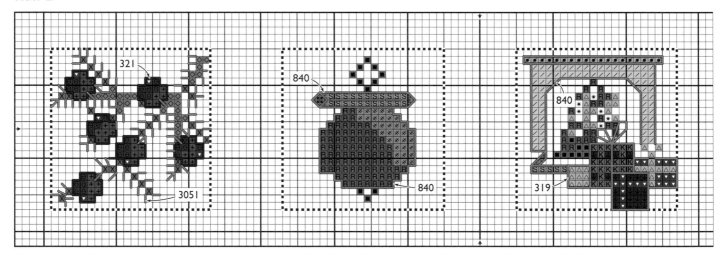

Row 3

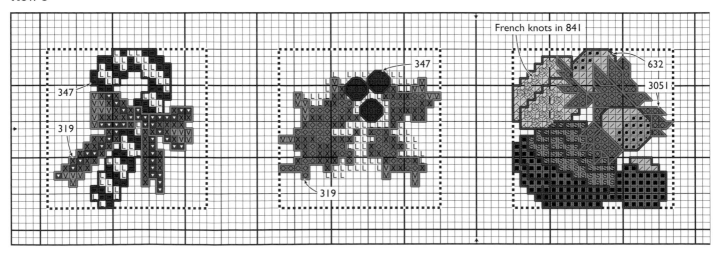

Row 1

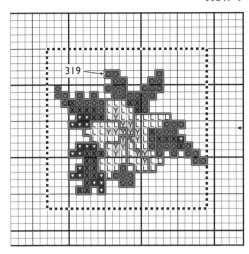

319

Row 2

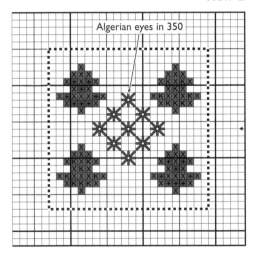

Algerian eyes in 350

Row 3

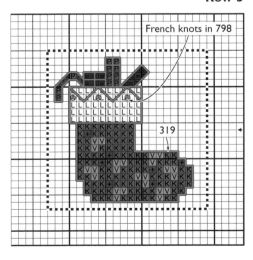

French knots in 798

319

SPARKLY ADVENT CALENDAR KEY
Stranded cotton (floss)

DMC	ANCHOR	BF = Blending Filament
319	382	
321	9046	+ Ver à Soie BF 003
327	94	+ Kreinik BF 026
347	9046	+ Ver à Soie BF 003
350	333	+ Ver à Soie BF 003
367	245	+ Kreinik BF 043
436	363	
437	891	
522	88	+ Kreinik BF 026
600	46	+ Ver à Soie BF 003
632	20	
676	301	+ Anchor Ophir 300
712	2	+ Kreinik Pearl BF
721	333	+ Kreinik BF 027
722	330	+ Kreinik BF 027
727	292	+ Kreinik BF 028
729	306	+ Kreinik BF 028
738	880	
741	298	+ Kreinik BF 027
742	303	+ Kreinik BF 027
743	289	+ Kreinik BF 028
798	131	+ Kreinik BF 033
799	1090	+ Kreinik BF 033
816	1006	
840	944	+ Kreinik BF 022
841	1046	+ Kreinik BF 022
3051	268	
3347	239	+ Kreinik BF 043
blanc	1	+ Kreinik Pearl BF
Madeira gold metallic		+ Madeira gold 22 (no.15)

Mill Hill Petite Glass Beads
42010 lustre

Row 4

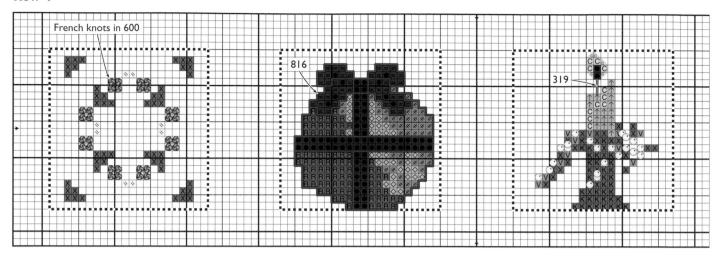

French knots in 600

816

319

Row 5

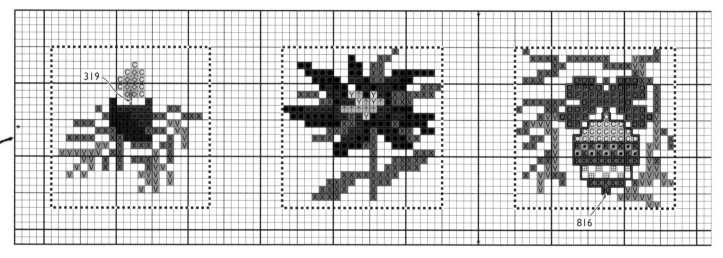

319

816

Row 6

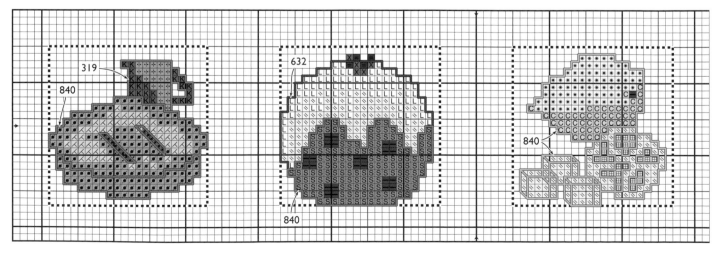

319

840

632

840

840

Row 4

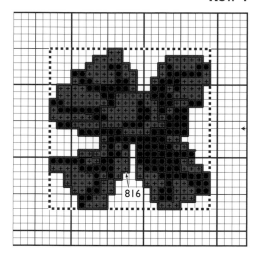

Row 5

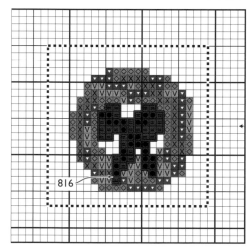

Row 6

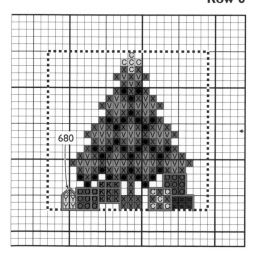

SPARKLY ADVENT CALENDAR KEY
Stranded cotton (floss)

	DMC	ANCHOR	BF = Blending Filament
	319	382	
	321	9046	+ Ver à Soie BF 003
	327	94	+ Kreinik BF 026
	347	9046	+ Ver à Soie BF 003
	350	333	+ Ver à Soie BF 003
	367	245	+ Kreinik BF 043
	436	363	
	437	891	
	522	88	+ Kreinik BF 026
	600	46	+ Ver à Soie BF 003
	632	20	
	676	301	+ Anchor Ophir 300
	712	2	+ Kreinik Pearl BF
	721	333	+ Kreinik BF 027
	722	330	+ Kreinik BF 027
	727	292	+ Kreinik BF 028
	729	306	+ Kreinik BF 028
	738	880	
	741	298	+ Kreinik BF 027
	742	303	+ Kreinik BF 027
	743	289	+ Kreinik BF 028
	798	131	+ Kreinik BF 033
	799	1090	+ Kreinik BF 033
	816	1006	
	840	944	+ Kreinik BF 022
	841	1046	+ Kreinik BF 022
	3051	268	
	3347	239	+ Kreinik BF 043
	blanc	1	+ Kreinik Pearl BF
	Madeira gold metallic		+ Madeira gold 22 (no.15)

Mill Hill Petite Glass Beads

42010 lustre

39

Beads, Buttons and Birds

This chapter explores some of the exciting embellishments you can use to enhance cross stitch designs. I show you how to use brilliant beads to add sparkle to your work, how to make buttons a focal point of designs and how to incorporate different stitches, such as bullion stitches and French knots, to produce interesting textures.

Substituting beads for cross stitch is explored in the gorgeous Beaded Bird and Bramble pillow, where hedgerow scenes, arranged as a garland, are embellished with seed beads and rustic wooden buttons. In the Button House sampler, a traditional design is transformed by the addition of a hand-crafted ceramic button. The charming Counting Sheep design is enhanced by the use of ceramic sheep buttons, both in the picture and bringing the frame to life too. These designs have also inspired three smaller card and gift tag projects, showing you how one element can be used as a focal point to create something new.

Embellishing cross stitch with beads and buttons will bring a new and eye-catching dimension to your stitching. There are a few rules to be observed, but the only real limit is your imagination.

CHAFFINCH GIFT CARD

Stitch count *29 x 33*

Design size
5 x 6.25cm (2 x 2½in)

This little chaffinch was stitched from the chart on page 47 on 14-count Aida using two strands of stranded cotton (floss) for cross stitch and one strand for backstitch. The fabric edges were frayed and the embroidery mounted on decorative paper.

BUTTERFLY GIFT TAG

Stitch count *19 x 14*

Design size *3.75 x 2.5cm (1½ x 1in)*

This charming little butterfly was stitched from the chart on page 47 on 14-count Yorkshire Aida, using two strands of stranded cotton (floss) for cross stitch and one strand for backstitch. The fabric was frayed up to the stitched area and mounted on silk paper with a decorative gold cord added.

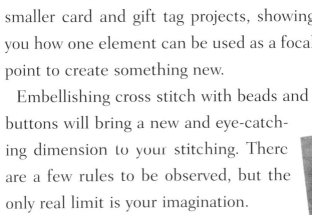

Beaded Bird and Bramble Garland

*T*o create extra texture this design was stitched in a combination of seed beads and cross stitch, with the addition of bullion stitches and French knots. It was worked on evenweave linen as the beads sit well on this type of fabric, but a 14-count Aida could also be used. Made up into a decorative pillow, the framing fabric and piping were chosen to enhance the colours in the design. Note: the caterpillar and bee have also been charted in cross stitch if you prefer not to use French knots or bullion stitches.

Stitch count

89 x 86

Design size

16 x 15.5cm (6½ x 6in)

YOU WILL NEED

29 x 28cm (11½ x 11in) Zweigart Cashel 28-count linen, shade 224

Tapestry needle size 26

Beading needle or size 10 sharp

Stranded cotton (floss) as listed in chart key

Stranded rayon thread as listed in chart key

Mill Hill beads as listed in chart key

Wooden birdhouse and butterfly buttons (Button Box, see Suppliers)

1 Fold the fabric in four and mark the folds with tacking (basting) stitches. Work the design from the chart on page 47, starting at the centre of the fabric and counting to the nearest cross stitch. Work over two fabric threads, using two strands of stranded cotton (floss) for cross stitch and one for backstitch.

2 Embellish the caterpillar (top left on chart) in bullion stitches and French knots (see Stitch Library pages 106 and 109) in the two rayon thread colours given. Work the bee in bullion stitches in the two rayon thread colours, with the wings, legs and antennae in backstitch.

3 To work the beaded sections, follow the chart, using a beading needle or very fine 'sharp' needle, and attach the seed beads using a half cross stitch and thread matching the background fabric. Each square on the chart indicates a bead and you can work across the pattern row by row (see technique panel, right, for advice on working with beads).

4 When all stitching and beading is complete, remove any tacking (basting), press on the wrong side and add the two wooden buttons using matching thread. Make your embroidery up into a cushion as described on page 118.

Counting Sheep

This charming picture is simply but effectively embellished by attaching a sheep button to the stitching with two more glued to the frame, with the illusion of being stitched in place. The sheep are worked in French knots, adding texture. The design could also be stitched on a 14-count Aida.

Stitch count

59 x 60

Design size

10.75 x 10.75cm

(4¼ x 4¼in)

YOU WILL NEED

20 x 20cm (8 x 8in)
Zweigart Cashel 28-
count linen, shade 224

Tapestry needle size 24

Stranded cotton (floss)
as listed in chart key

Three hand-crafted
sheep buttons (Terata,
see Suppliers)

Craft glue

Tip

When using buttons,
ensure that the button
size is appropriate for
the project, matching
the size with the cross
stitch motifs used.

1 Fold the fabric in four and mark the folds with tacking (basting) stitches. Work the design, starting at the centre of the chart on page 46 and the centre of the fabric. Work over two fabric threads, using two strands of stranded cotton (floss) for cross stitch and one for backstitch. Use random French knots in two strands of white and black to create the sheep shapes shown on the chart.

2 When finished, press the embroidery carefully on the wrong side, then attach the sheep button with matching thread. Mount and frame as a picture (see page 116). Before gluing the other two buttons on to the frame, sew through them to give the impression that they are stitched in place.

WORKING WITH BEADS

Substituting beads for embroidery cotton (floss) is very easy and a wonderful way to add dimension, texture and sparkle.

● Working with beads is easier than you can imagine: as all the beads are stitched on using only one colour thread, you can work across the pattern row by row instead of working blocks of colour as for cross stitch.

● There are dozens of different shapes, sizes and colours of bead available. Do, however, choose 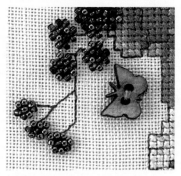 beads suitable for your fabric count. If the beads are too large the design will distort and the beads will crowd on top of each other. Most seed beads are perfect for 14-count fabric or canvas (28 threads per 2.5cm/1in).

● Choose your fabric with care when incorporating beads. Although beads can be used on any fabric, they will sit better on evenweave than Aida and on double canvas than on single.

● Consider using a frame or hoop when working with beads. This will keep the fabric taut and you can pull the thread firmly as you work to keep the beads in position.

● Attach beads using ordinary sewing thread which matches the fabric colour, a beading needle or very fine 'sharp' needle and a half cross stitch. To make sure that you can't see the thread through the beads, attach a few to 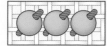 a corner of the fabric to check.

Button House Sampler

This simply stitched, traditional sampler is brought to life with the addition of a single embellishment – an attractive ceramic, house-shaped button. If you prefer, the design could easily be worked on a 16-count Aida instead of the 32-count linen.

Stitch count	Design size
61 x 83	*9.75 x 13.25cm*
	(3¾ x 5¼in)

YOU WILL NEED

19.5 x 23.5cm (7¾ x 9¼in) Zweigart Belfast 32-count linen, shade 224

Tapestry needle size 24

Stranded cotton (floss) as listed in chart key

Hand-crafted house button (Terata, see Suppliers)

PARCHMENT PAPER CARD

Stitch count *32 x 32*

Design size *5.75 x 5.75cm (2¼ x 2¼in)*

Make a gift card using motifs from the Button House sampler. Cross stitch with three strands of stranded cotton on 14 holes per 2.5cm (1in) stitching paper. Once stitched, mark the centre and draw diagonal lines out over eight holes. Cut along the lines and fold back the points, tinting them with a gold pen. Stick the stitching to a piece of card, stitching the house button in the centre. Use decorative scissors for a pretty edging.

1 Fold the fabric in four and mark the folds with tacking (basting) stitches. Work the design from the centre of the chart and fabric, counting to the nearest cross stitch. Working over two fabric threads, use two strands of stranded cotton (floss) for cross stitches.

2 When the embroidery is complete, remove any tacking (basting). Use matching thread to stitch on the house button in the centre above the heart motif, and then mount and frame your work as a picture (see page 116).

Tip

Take care that buttons, particularly wooden ones, do not mark your fabric. If unsure, coat the back with a clear nail varnish before attaching them.

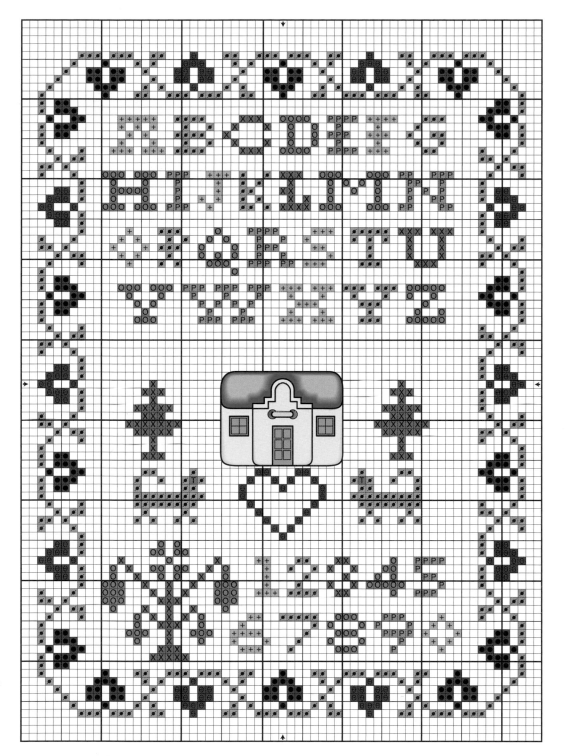

**BUTTON HOUSE
SAMPLER KEY
Stranded cotton (floss)**

	DMC	ANCHOR
	223	10
	315	65
	420	1049
	832	307
	926	208
	930	1036
	3011	277
	3041	1018

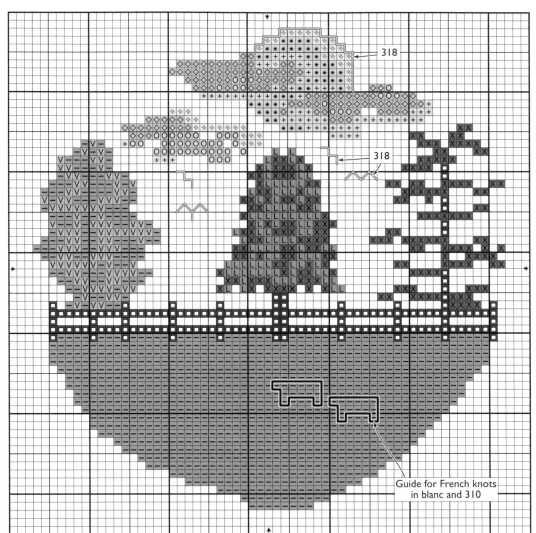

COUNTING SHEEP KEY
Stranded cotton (floss)

	DMC	ANCHOR
■	310	403
▨	318	232
▨	367	245
▤	470	256
⋁	471	279
+	543	1026
▦	632	20
✻	676	301
▨	677	386
○	842	387
L	3347	239

French knots

❀	blanc	1
❀	310	403

318

318

Guide for French knots
in blanc and 310

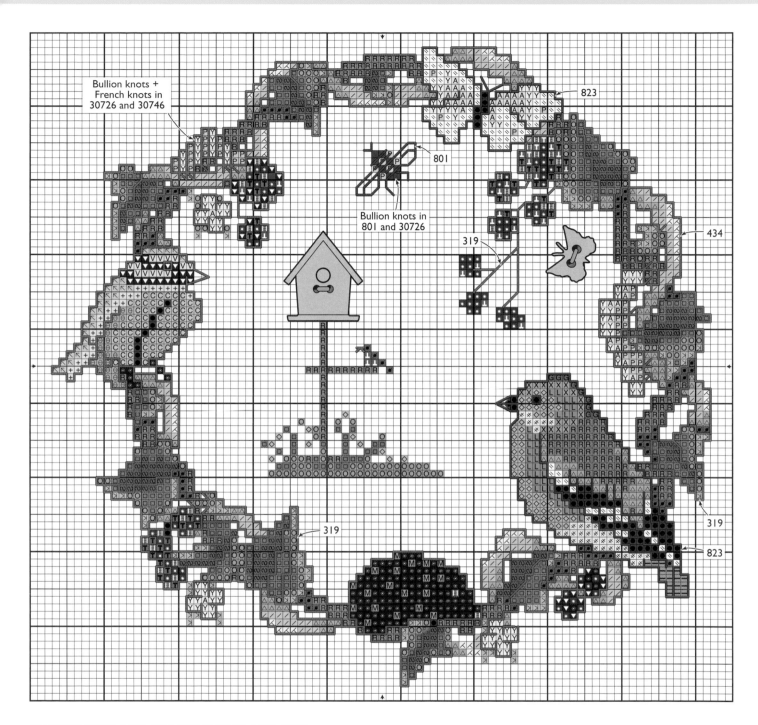

Bullion knots +
French knots in
30726 and 30746

801

Bullion knots in
801 and 30726

823

434

319

319

823

319

BEADED BIRD AND BRAMBLE GARLAND KEY
Stranded cotton (floss)

DMC	ANCHOR		DMC	ANCHOR		DMC	ANCHOR		Mill Hill Beads	
434	351		712	2		319	879	Backstitch only	0020	00146
435	308		738	926		801	381	Bullions + backstitch	02011	00168
436	363		754	271					03033	00374
437	891		758	36		Rayon à Broder 30726			00367	03038
469	268		807	186		Rayon à Broder 30746			02011	02002
470	256		823	403					02014	00252
471	279		937	269						
640	374		3760	142						
676	301		3778	329						

Charmed Cross Stitch

There are some wonderful charms available today and choosing the right 'exciting embellishment' to enhance an embroidery design is great fun. Charms can form an important part of the design, either attached to the fabric, secured on top of cross stitch motifs or taking the place of a stitched motif completely.

There are charms in practically every shape you could wish for – birds, bees, butterflies, hearts, flowers, rabbits, snails, four-leafed clovers! They are also made from many different materials including metal, ceramic, wood, paper, raffia – look in your local craft shops and the craft magazines for ideas.

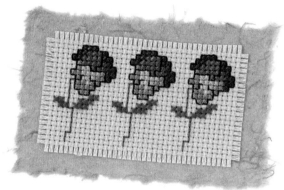

Some care needs to be taken when attaching charms: the production of brass charms involves the use of strong chemicals which, if still present on the back of the charm, can mark embroideries permanently, especially if the stitching is exposed to a damp atmosphere. A scouring method is used to clean good quality charms for use on embroidery, which prevents potential damage (see also the useful tip on page 52).

The Violet and Pansy Charm samplers featured in this section both use charms to great effect, their purple, blue and lilac colouring attractively complemented by the brass charms. The anniversary sampler is further embellished by the inclusion of pulled satin stitch and Greek cross stitch – pulled stitches that are simple to work and produce a pretty, lacy effect on evenweave fabric. Two lovely little cards have also been created using motifs from the charm sampler chart.

VIOLET TRIO

Stitch count 36 x 20

Design size 6.5 x 3.75cm
(2¾ x 1½in)

This sweet little card uses the violets from the chart on page 51. It was cross stitched on 14-count grey Aida using two strands of stranded cotton (floss) for cross stitch and one strand for backstitch. The design was cut and frayed to within two squares of the stitching and mounted on plain white card covered with torn green paper.

Violet and Pansy Charm Sampler

This lovely sampler is very easy to stitch, its charming antique appearance created by working subtle colours on unbleached linen. Because it uses only cross stitch and backstitch you could also work the design on 14-count Aida. The size of the insect charms has been chosen to be in proportion to the design.

Stitch count
94 x 98

Design size
17 x 18cm (6¾ x 7in)

YOU WILL NEED

30.5 x 30.5cm (12 x 12in) Zweigart Cashel 28-count unbleached linen, shade 53

Tapestry needle size 24

Stranded cottons (floss) as listed in chart key

Four brass bee charms and one gold butterfly (CSG, see Suppliers)

1 Fold the fabric in four and mark the folds with tacking (basting) stitches. Work the design from the centre of the chart and the centre of the fabric. Work over two fabric threads, starting with a loop start (see page 8) and using two strands of stranded cotton (floss) for cross stitch and three-quarter cross stitch and one strand for backstitching.

2 Using matching thread, stitch the little insect charms to the four corners as marked on the chart (see Tip below). Stitch the gold butterfly in position above the heart motif.

3 When the stitching is complete, check for missed stitches, remove tacking (basting) and frame as a picture (see page 116).

Tip

Attach charms and buttons using a thread matching the fabric. Starting with a loop start, position the charm and pass the needle through the hole from the right side thus marking the position. Stitch in position carefully, ensuring that the threads on the needle stay taut and do not form an unsightly loop in the hole in the charm.

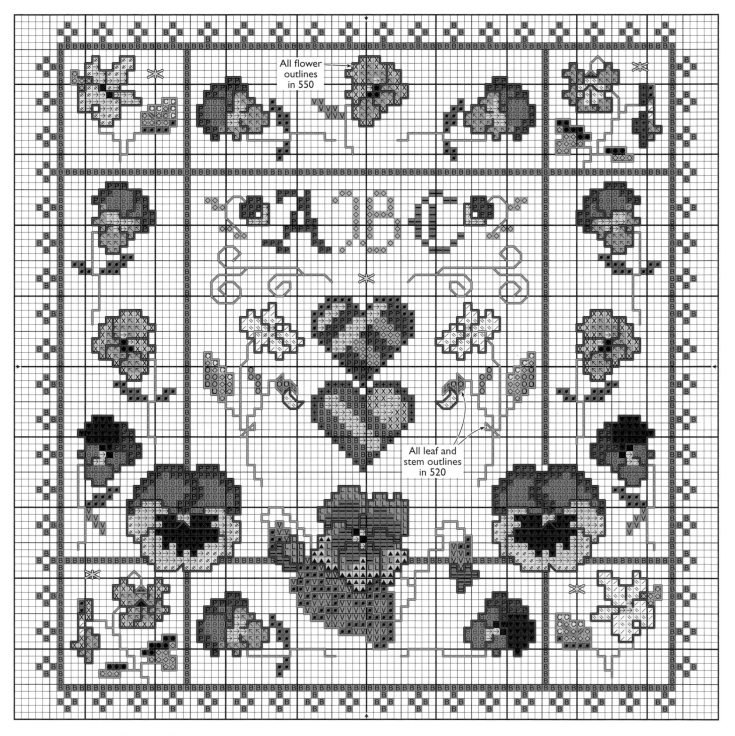

All flower outlines in 550

All leaf and stem outlines in 520

VIOLET AND PANSY CHARM SAMPLER KEY
Stranded cotton (floss)

DMC	ANCHOR		DMC	ANCHOR		DMC	ANCHOR		DMC	ANCHOR		DMC	ANCHOR
310	403		520	382		553	86		3346	245		blanc	1
333	111		522	261		676	301		3347	239			
340	120		524	259		677	386		3834	972		Charm positions	
341	1096		550	102		712	2		3836	390			
470	256		552	88		931	978		3835	1018			

Pansy and Violet Anniversary Sampler

This delicate anniversary sampler uses the chart on page 51, but omits the border and the solid lines dividing the motifs. Some pulled thread embroidery has been added, including Greek cross stitch, pulled satin stitch and eyelets, plus a hemstitched border. If you intend to include the pulled thread work, this design can only be worked on evenweave.

Stitch count

84 x 89 (excluding hemstitched border)

Design size

15.25 x 16cm
(6 x 6½in)

YOU WILL NEED

28 x 28cm (11 x 11in) Zweigart Cashel 28-count linen in antique white

Tapestry needle size 24

Stranded cottons (floss) as listed in chart key

Two antique gold-coloured heart charms (see CSG, Suppliers)

Tip

If you are concerned about the finish on a charm marking your work, paint the back of it with clear nail varnish and leave to dry before use.

1 Fold the fabric in four and mark the folds with tacking (basting) stitches. Work over two fabric threads from the chart on page 51 but omit the blue border, blue lines, white flowers, backstitch motif and the lower heart. Start at the centre of the fabric with a loop start (see page 8). Use two strands of stranded cotton (floss) for cross stitch and three-quarter cross stitch and one strand for backstitch.

2 For the centre of the design, refer to the chart detail on page 54 to work the heart outline in cross stitch in 333 or a colour of your choice, leaving the inside un-stitched for the moment. Cross stitch your own initials and date in the grey areas, using the alphabet and numbers provided. It is best to plan your letters and numbers on squared paper first so that they can be placed and stitched in the correct positions.

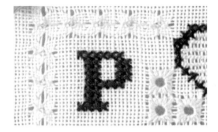

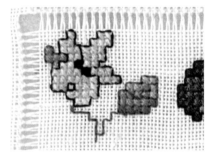

3 To create the lacy effect of the centre panel, use two strands of 712 stranded cotton (floss) and work Greek cross stitches where shown on the chart, pulling the stitches firmly (see technique panel, right).

4 Using two strands of 712 stranded cotton (floss), fill the heart motif with pulled satin stitches (see technique panel on page 55) working in two directions, as shown in the picture detail, left. Add three eyelets (see technique panel on page 55) on either side of the heart with two strands of 712. Stitch on the two heart charms with matching thread to finish.

5 To add a hemstitch border, count out two threads from the stitching and withdraw four threads from one side, re-weaving into the border as described on page 28. Repeat around the other three sides prior to adding a row of hemstitches around the outside edge only.

6 When all the stitching has been completed, check for missed stitches, remove any tacking (basting) and frame (see page 116 for mounting and framing).

WORKING GREEK CROSS STITCH

This lacy stitch creates a delicate pattern that is simple to work but very effective. It can also be used as a filling stitch.

● Bring the needle and thread through at 1, go down at 2 (four threads up and four to the right) and then up at 3 (four threads down), keeping the thread under the needle.

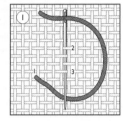

● Pull the thread through then put the needle down at 4 (four threads to the right) and up at 3 as shown (four threads to left), keeping the thread under the needle.

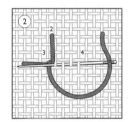

● Pull the thread through then put the needle down at 5 (four threads down) and up at 3 (four threads up), keeping the thread under the needle.

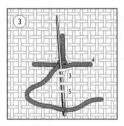

● Pull the thread through and secure the cross by inserting the needle at 3 to overlap the first and last stitches.

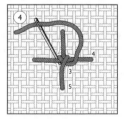

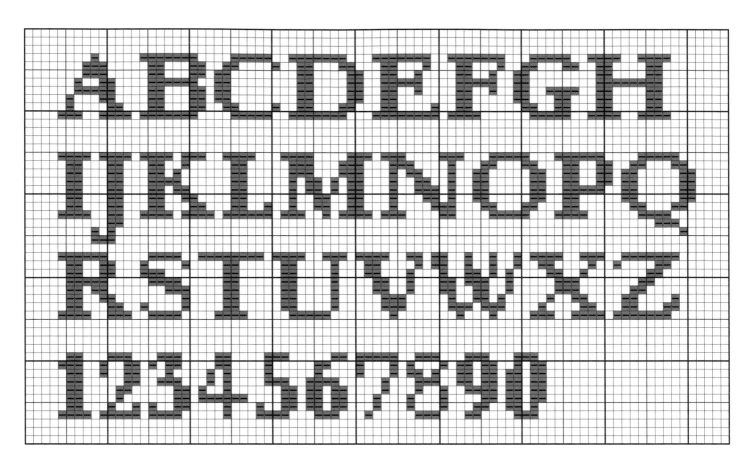

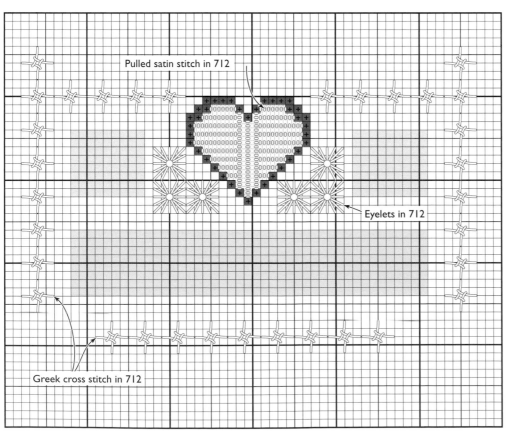

Pulled satin stitch in 712

Eyelets in 712

Greek cross stitch in 712

**PANSY AND VIOLET
ANNIVERSARY
SAMPLER (CENTRAL PART)
KEY**

Stranded cotton (floss)

DMC	ANCHOR
3834	972
333	111
712	2

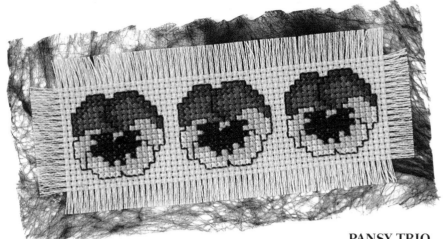

PANSY TRIO

Stitch count 54 x 15

Design size 10 x 2.5cm (4 x 1in)

This pretty card uses the chart on page 51 and was cross stitched on 14-count grey Aida using two strands of stranded cotton (floss) for cross stitch and one for backstitch. The design was cut and frayed to within two squares of the stitching and mounted on plain white card covered with purple silk paper.

WORKING EYELETS AND PULLED SATIN STITCH

Both of these stitches are used in the anniversary sampler to create visual interest.

EYELETS

These can be stitched in various shapes (see Stitch Library page 108) and the rules are the same for all eyelets: as with Algerian eye you need to pass the needle down the central hole, working the stitch in the correct sequence and in one direction to ensure that the hole is round and uniform. Take care that trailing threads do not cover the hole as you progress to the next stitch. Square eyelets are used in the Pansy and Violet Anniversary Sampler (page 52) and star-shaped eyelets in the Sea Breezes band sampler (page 26).

PULLED SATIN STITCH

This simple stitch forms holes in the fabric that look very effective. It is worked in the same way as normal satin stitch but pulling the thread as you stitch

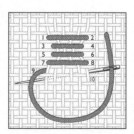

forms holes in the fabric and creates a different, lacier effect.

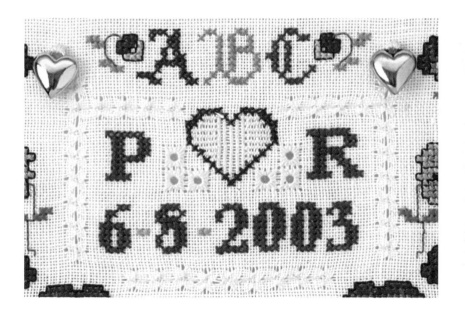

Needlelace Flowers

*A*s a self-confessed counted embroidery addict, cross stitch is still my favourite type of embroidery and I just love the effect that can be achieved with pure cross stitch and colour shading. Having said that, I think that it is sometimes very effective to add a little three-dimensional effect to some designs. This can be done with the addition of French knots, bullion stitches or beads. This chapter uses all of those and also shows you how to create needlelace flowers, an attractive technique used in samplers as far back as the 17th century.

I gain much inspiration from past treasures, particularly when designing. For the curious amongst you, I thought you might like to know that the metal item hanging to the right of the sampler pictured here is a chatelaine dated about 1790. It would have been attached to the waistband of the mistress of the house, or the housekeeper, and it includes an *aide-memoire*, a pincushion, a tape measure, some scissors and a small coin purse.

The project featured in this chapter is a sampler that has links with the past but breaks the rules, just a little. It is not symmetrical and the flowers within the border are all slightly different. It also has an attractive three-dimensional quality achieved by the addition of needlelace petals, bullion stitches and beads on some of the roses.

I have used various motifs from the chart on pages 62/63 to create three smaller projects, all worked on 14-count Aida – a pink flower bookmark, a heart and flower card and a beaded briar rose card. There's also a pretty case I've called a stitcher's floral companion. It's worked on 28-count linen and features double faggot stitch – something a little different to try.

BEADED BRIAR ROSE CARD

Stitch count 31 x 30

Design size 5.5 x 5.5cm (2¼ x 2¼in)

The rose was cross stitched on 14-count cream Aida using two strands of stranded cotton (floss) for cross stitch and one for backstitch. Small pearl seed beads were added to the flower centre using a beading needle and a half cross stitch. The card was then trimmed to within five squares of the stitching and frayed. It was mounted on to a handmade card covered in dolls' house wallpaper.

Needlelace Flower Sampler

The lovely needlelace petals on this sampler (shown on page 57) aren't difficult to do but you might find it helpful to work a few on spare fabric before beginning to embellish your stitching. If you prefer you could cross stitch the flower centres instead (a separate chart gives an example). You could also repeat the corner versions of the roses, with bullion stitches and glass beads instead of needlelace.

Stitch count *128 x 162*

Design size *23.25 x 30cm (9 x 11½in)*

YOU WILL NEED

35.5 x 43cm (14 x 17in) Cashel 28-count linen, shade 222

Tapestry needle size 24

Beading needle or size 10 sharp

Stranded cotton (floss) as listed in chart key

Perlé cotton No 12 ecru

Mill Hill Petite glass beads, gold (40557)

1 Fold the fabric in four and mark the folds with tacking (basting) stitches. Start stitching in the middle of the fabric to ensure adequate space for finishing. Work the design over two fabric threads from the centre of the chart on pages 62/63, completing all cross stitching before adding any of the other stitches. Use two strands of stranded cotton (floss) for the cross stitches, three-quarter cross stitches and French knots. Add backstitches in one strand.

2 With two strands of 712 add bullion stitches (see page 106) to the four corner flower centres (see picture below) using a gold-plated needle if you have one. Add the beads to the centre of the bullion stitches using one strand of stranded cotton (floss), a half cross stitch and a sharp or beading needle. Add random French knots to the centres of the smaller pink flowers with two strands of 930.

3 To work the needlelace petals, see picture below and refer to the technique panel, right. These petals use one strand of ecru perlé cotton No 12 but could be worked in stranded cotton with great effect. (Refer to the separately charted rose on page 63 if you prefer to use cross stitch and French knots in the centres.)

4 When the stitching is complete, check for missed stitches, remove any tacking (basting) and frame as a picture (see page 116).

HEART AND FLOWER CARD

Stitch count *35 x 60*

Design size *6.5 x 11cm (2½ x 4¼in)*

This pretty card uses motifs from the chart on pages 62/63 and was cross stitched on 14-count Aida using two strands of stranded cotton (floss) for cross stitch and one for backstitch. The stitching was mounted on to handmade paper and card using double-sided adhesive tape.

Designing cards such as this one is an excellent way to gain confidence as a new designer as you can see the end result quickly. You can take motifs from the charts in this book and produce very effective designs. The secret is to keep records – keep a clean copy of any original card but write notes on the working chart. Keep notes simple, e.g., 'French knots here'. The colours and details can be added as you stitch. It is important to keep records of colours used because you will not believe how difficult it is to work out later! Avoid adding too many colours to a pattern but use different shades of the same colour, e.g., DMC 367, 368 and 369 are complementary shades of green and would count as one colour addition.

CREATING NEEDLELACE FLOWERS

Needlelace flowers are not a modern idea – some samplers from the 17th century included pretty flower petals created this way. The technique isn't difficult but practising on spare fabric would be helpful before starting your sampler.

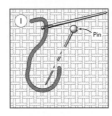

● Begin by positioning a glass-headed pin in the material as shown in Fig 1. If using stranded cotton (floss), anchor a pair of threads using the loop start method. (Use one strand if using perlé cotton.)

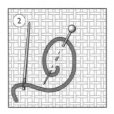 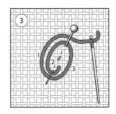

● Wind the thread around the pin as in Fig 2 and then around again as in Fig 3.

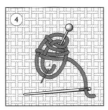

● When you are at the head of the pin, stop winding and, using the needle, weave in and out of the threads as in Fig 4. It takes a little practice to get an even finish but it is very effective.

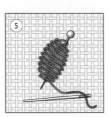

● When a petal is complete, pass the needle to the wrong side of the work and remove the pin. Repeat the process to make as many petals as you need.

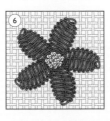

● When the flower is complete, add some French knots randomly to the centre using two strands of thread.

● When creating needlelace petals you can alter the shape as you stitch. The petal or leaves may look pointed or have rounded ends depending on how firmly you push each weave towards the beginning of the petal. Experiment and you will surprise yourself.

Stitcher's Floral Companion

This pretty little case (shown on page 57) is the perfect chance for you to create your own design using motifs from the main chart on pages 62–63. Remember, you can turn the chart around to have motifs facing in different directions or even use a mirror to create a reverse image.

Stitch count

80 x 55

(excluding border)

Design size

14.5 x 10cm

(5¾ x 4in)

YOU WILL NEED

30.5 x 58.5cm (12 x 23in) Zweigart Cashel 28-count linen, shade 638

Tapestry needle size 24

Stranded cotton (floss) as listed in chart key

1 Lay the fabric on to a clean surface with the narrow edge towards you. Fold the material into three sections and mark each fold with a pin. Fold the top section into four and mark the folds with tacking (basting) stitches. This section will be the front flap featuring your design.

2 Using the chart, begin to stitch the motifs (or choose your own combination) over two fabric threads, starting at the centre of the fabric. Use two strands of stranded cotton (floss) for cross stitch and three-quarter cross stitch and one strand for backstitch.

3 To add your initials, first copy the letters from the chart on to squared paper and mark the centre. You will then be able to place the initials in the correct place on the fabric.

4 To create a stitched framing border, work one row of four-sided stitch (page 108) over four threads around the design using two strands of the darkest green stranded cotton (floss). The lacy effect is achieved by working double faggot stitch (see technique panel, right, and the stitching detail below) and a few random Algerian eyes (see page 106) using two strands of 712 and referring to the photograph on page 57. To create the fold of the case, count up twenty-four threads from the top row of the frame and work a row of four-sided stitch across the width of the project.

5 When the stitching is complete, check for missed stitches, remove any tacking (basting) and make up into a case with a bias binding edging (see pages 117 and 119).

PINK FLOWER BOOKMARK

Stitch count 21 x 40

Design size 4 x 7.25cm (1½ x 2⅞in)

This bookmark was cross stitched on 14-count Aida using two strands of stranded cotton (floss) for cross stitch and one strand for backstitch. The embroidery was then cut to within two squares of the stitching, frayed and mounted on to handmade paper.

WORKING DOUBLE FAGGOT STITCH

This stitch creates textured areas in a design and can be worked as a border or in a regular pattern for filling in larger areas.

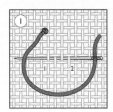

● Starting with an away waste knot, bring the thread through the fabric at 1, then insert the needle at 2 (four threads to the right) and bring through at 1 again. Remember to pull firmly to create the holes.

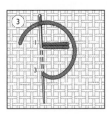

● Re-insert the needle at 2, then bring it through at 3 (four threads down and four to the left).

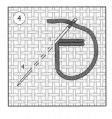

● Insert the needle at 1 (four threads up) and bring it through at 3 again.

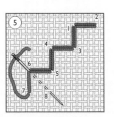

● Re-insert the needle at 1, then bring it through at 4 (four threads down and four to the left).

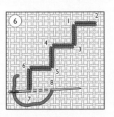

● Continue in this way, following the number sequence to the end of the row. Complete the last stitch 7–8 by re-inserting the needle in 6 and bringing it out at 8 (four threads down and four to the right). Turn the work around to work the last row.

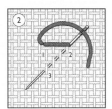

● Bring the thread through at 8, then insert the needle at 7 and through at 8 again. Turn the work and repeat the procedure to create four sides to each stitch. Cut off the away waste knot and re-thread the needle, weaving the thread through the back of the work.

Needlelace petals in perlé cotton No 12 in ecru

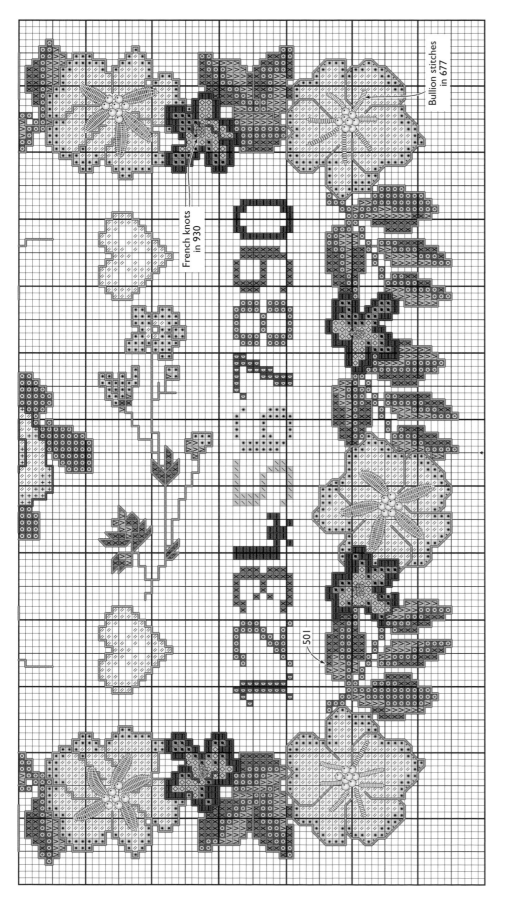

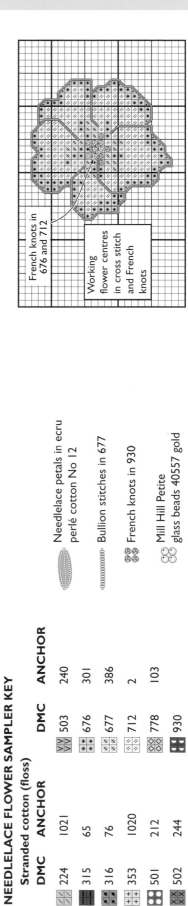

French knots in 676 and 712

Working flower centres in cross stitch and French knots

Bullion stitches in 677

French knots in 930

501

NEEDLELACE FLOWER SAMPLER KEY

Stranded cotton (floss)

	DMC	ANCHOR		DMC	ANCHOR
	224	1021		503	240
	315	65		676	301
	316	76		677	386
	353	1020		712	2
	501	212		778	103
	502	244		930	

Needlelace petals in ecru perlé cotton No 12

Bullion stitches in 677

French knots in 930

Mill Hill Petite glass beads 40557 gold

Beautiful Blackwork

Blackwork is an embroidery technique consisting of geometric patterns built up using Holbein stitch (also called double running stitch) and was traditionally worked in black thread against a contrasting (usually white) background with gold metallic highlights added for extra impact. In Tudor times, blackwork designs were often made up of scrolls of vine leaves and bunches of grapes, filled in with various patterns. The stems and outlines were always worked in a heavier stitch. During the Elizabethan period blackwork embroidery was used to decorate clothing to imitate the appearance of lace although the name is a little misleading as this type of counted embroidery can be stitched in any colour, as you can see from the designs in this chapter!

Holbein stitch is so-called because patterns worked this way appear in many of the pictures of the painter Hans Holbein (1497–1543), decorating the clothes of people in his portraits.

Holbein stitch produces a smooth effect and the back of your work will look almost as good as the front, so it is particularly useful for table linen. Many different effects can be achieved by varying the thickness of the threads used, and careful selection of patterns with dark, medium and light tones. You will see from my Blackwork Beasts picture that you can choose different patterns to produce the dark and light effects. The design has also been used to create two smaller projects – a stylish owl notebook cover and a cute hedgehog card.

OWL NOTEBOOK

Stitch count 37 x 46

*Design size 7 x 8.5cm
(2¾ x 3¼in)*

The owl and acorn from the main chart were stitched on 14-count cream Aida, using two strands of stranded cotton (floss) shade DMC 840 for the outline and one strand for the filling pattern, with Madeira Gold No 15 shade 22 to highlight. The acorn motif was stitched in DMC 320. The back of the design was painted with PVA glue and allowed to dry. The design was cut out, leaving one row of fabric squares. The motif was then stuck to the front of a notebook using double-sided adhesive tape.

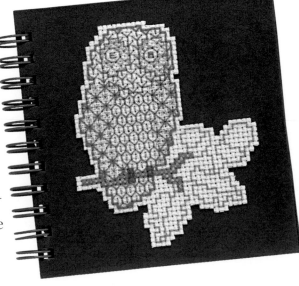

Blackwork Beasts

I have always enjoyed blackwork because it has an impressive look about it yet is created so simply. It need not be worked in black and gold and can look very effective in red, green or dark blue. Many cross stitch charts can be converted into blackwork by using the existing outline and a variety of black-work filling stitches. Generally, blackwork designs are of a floral nature so I thought beasts would make a change! I have completed this project as a picture but it would also make a sumptuous cushion.

Stitch count
192 x 172

Design size
35 x 31.25cm
(13¾ x 12¼in)

YOU WILL NEED

48 x 43cm (19 x 17in)
28-count Zweigart
Cashel linen, shade 101

Tapestry needle size 24

Stranded cottons (floss)
as listed in chart key

Madeira No 15 gold
metallic shade 22

1 Fold the fabric in four and mark the folds with tacking (basting) stitches. Work in Holbein stitch over two fabric threads from the chart, starting at the centre of the fabric and chart. Use two strands of stranded cotton (floss) for overall outlines and blackwork section outlines and one strand for the filling stitches. Use the metallic gold straight from the reel.

2 Work the snail first as it's the central design, referring to the technique panel opposite and completing the blackwork in stages as described there.

3 When all the stitching is complete, check for missed stitches, remove any tacking (basting) and then mount and frame as a picture (see page 116).

HEDGEHOG CARD

Stitch count 45 x 23

Design size 8 x 4.25cm (3¼ x 1¾in)

This endearing little hedgehog from the main chart was stitched on to 14-count Aida fabric using two strands of stranded cotton (floss) for the outline and one strand for the filling patterns. Highlighting was added in Madeira Gold No 15 shade 22, with the foreground worked in backstitch in DMC 367. The design was then frayed to within two squares of the stitching and stuck to a piece of handmade paper and pressed flower card trimmed with raffia.

Tip
Before starting to stitch, plan the direction in which you intend to work so that you can return to fill the gaps without ending up a blind alley

BUILDING UP BLACKWORK

Traditionally, blackwork designs are worked by stitching the motif outline first, usually in a thicker thread, and then filling in the various sections with filling patterns, starting in the centre of each section and working outwards.

● Chart 1 – work the outline of the snail in Holbein stitch using two strands of stranded cotton (see main chart key for colours).

● Charts 2 & 3 – work the first blackwork pattern in Holbein stitch in two places on the snail, using one strand.

● Chart 4 – work the second pattern, using one strand of gold thread for the yellow stitches.

● Chart 5 – work the third pattern, adding the gold pattern with one strand.

● Chart 6 – once all the blackwork patterns are complete, add the grass in green half cross stitch.

WORKING HOLBEIN STITCH

This stitch, also called double running stitch, creates a smooth appearance and is simple to work.

● Work a row of Holbein stitch in one direction and then work back over the row in the opposite direction, filling in the gaps.

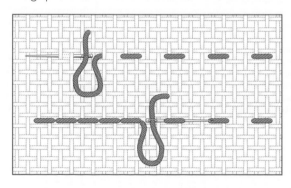

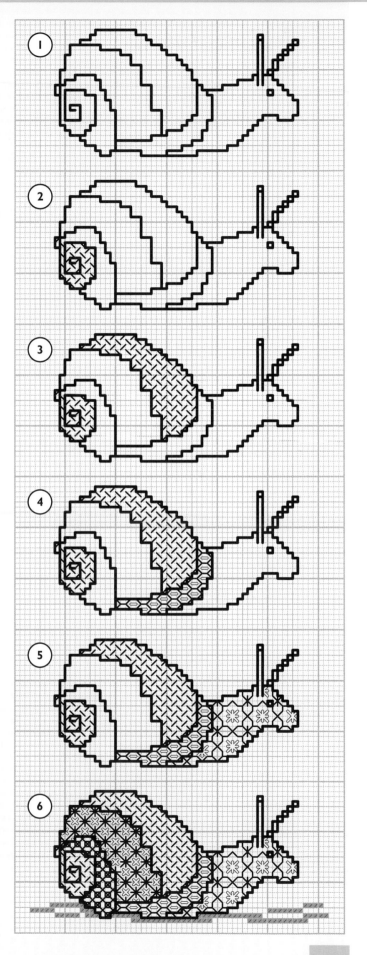

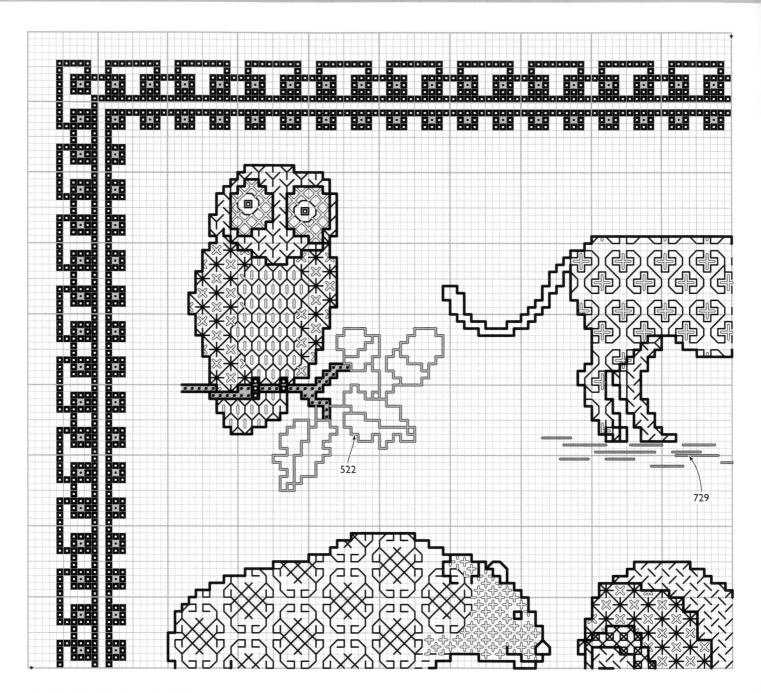

522

729

BLACKWORK BEASTS KEY

Stranded cotton (floss)

DMC	ANCHOR		DMC	ANCHOR	
310	403		310	403	2 strands, Holbein stitch (animal outlines)
317	878		310	403	1 strand, Holbein stitch (filling patterns)
blanc	1		Madeira gold metallic		2 strands, Holbein stitch
320	226 (half cross stitch)				
Madeira gold metallic					

320

320

BLACKWORK BEASTS KEY

Stranded cotton (floss)

DMC	ANCHOR		DMC	ANCHOR	
310	403		310	403	2 strands, Holbein stitch (animal outlines)
317	878		310	403	1 strand, Holbein stitch (filling patterns)
blanc	1		Madeira gold metallic		2 strands, Holbein stitch
320	226 (half cross stitch)				
Madeira gold metallic					

320

320

522

522

522

Hardanger Hearts

Hardanger embroidery is quite straightforward to do and extremely effective when combined with cross stitch. At its simplest, Hardanger work consists of three stages – stitching Kloster blocks, cutting threads and decorating the remaining threads and spaces. The secret of successful cutwork embroidery is working Kloster blocks accurately (the framework needed for the decorative filling stitches) and to count these blocks correctly. If they are in the *right* place the threads can be cut out and the stitching will *not* fall to pieces! Hardanger embroidery can be worked on evenweave fabric of any count or on Hardanger fabric which is supplied with 22 blocks to 2.5cm (1in) and where each block is treated as one thread.

The main project in this section is the Honeysuckle and Hardanger Hearts picture, shown on page 76, which is the perfect opportunity to practise your Hardanger skills as it features beautiful cross stitched honeysuckle surrounded by varied Hardanger motifs. If you prefer, you could begin with the lovely wedding ring pillow, shown right. This has a single Hardanger heart above a small spray of honeysuckle. There is also a pretty beaded honeysuckle card – perfect for a special occasion.

BEADED HONEYSUCKLE CARD

Stitch count 34 x 23

Design size 6 x 4cm
(2½ x 1½in)

This pretty little design was adapted from the chart on page 75. It was stitched over two threads of 28-count Cashel linen, shade 558, though it could also be worked over one block of a 14-count Aida. Two strands of stranded cotton (floss) were used for cross stitch and one strand for backstitch. Mill Hill glass seed beads shade 40123 were stitched on to each stamen. The design was cut out and frayed to within one square of the stitching, then mounted on a piece of handmade paper and a plain card with a ribbon trim.

Honeysuckle Ring Pillow

This charming little cushion was designed as a wedding ring pillow but could also be made up as a scented sachet or a framed picture. Your initials can be added using the charted alphabet.

Stitch count
46 x 60 (including four-sided stitch)

Design size
8.25 x 11cm (3¼ x 4¼in)

YOU WILL NEED

20 x 25.5cm (8 x 10in) white 27-count Jobelan

Tapestry needles sizes 24 and 22

Beading needle or size 10 sharp

Stranded cottons (floss) as listed in chart key

Anchor Multicolour pearl cotton 1335

Perlé cotton No 12 ecru

Mill Hill Petite glass beads, pearl (40123)

1 Fold the fabric in four and mark the folds with tacking (basting) stitches. Work the design from the chart, starting at the centre of the fabric. Work the cross stitch over two fabric threads, beginning with a loop start (page 8). Use two strands of stranded cotton (floss) for cross stitch and one for backstitch.

2 Work the Kloster blocks for the Hardanger heart using one strand of Anchor Multi-colour pearl cotton 1335 (see technique panel, right, and page 82 for using variegated thread).

3 Once the Kloster blocks have been cut, work the needleweaving and the dove's eye stitches using one strand of ecru perlé cotton No 12 (see Stitch Library, pages 112 and 113).

4 Add the beads as shown on the chart, using a beading needle and a half cross stitch.

5 When the stitching is complete, check for missed stitches, remove tacking (basting) and make up as a cushion (see page 118).

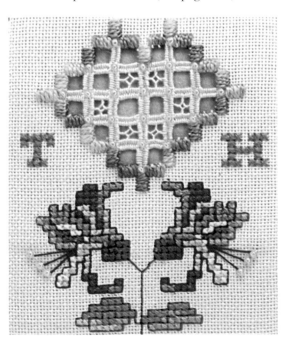

WORKING KLOSTER BLOCKS

Hardanger embroidery is distinguished by its cutwork and Kloster blocks form the frame-work for these cut areas.

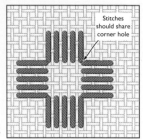

● Using one strand of ecru perlé cotton No 8, form Kloster blocks with 5 verti-cal or 5 horizontal straight stitches, each of them over 4 threads on evenweave or 4 blocks if working on Hardanger fabric. Keep checking that the blocks are directly opposite each other. The vertical and horizontal blocks must meet at the corners and share the same corner hole.

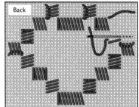

● If the stitches are worked side by side they will appear on the back of the fabric as here. Make sure that you do *not* travel between Kloster blocks at the back unless under existing blocks.

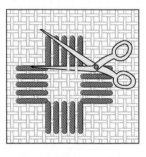

● When all the blocks are complete and match every-where, use sharp, pointed scissors to cut across the ends of the blocks. Take this slowly, counting and cutting two threads each time, starting from a shared corner hole. Try to cut in the same direction each time, turning the work as necessary. (See also the small chart on page 79 as an example of which threads may be cut.)

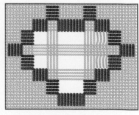

● Once the threads are cut, withdraw them, leaving the cutwork area ready for needleweaving, wrapped bars and filling stitches.

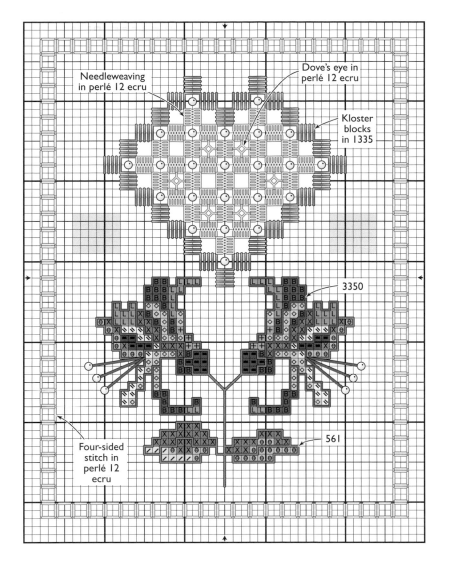

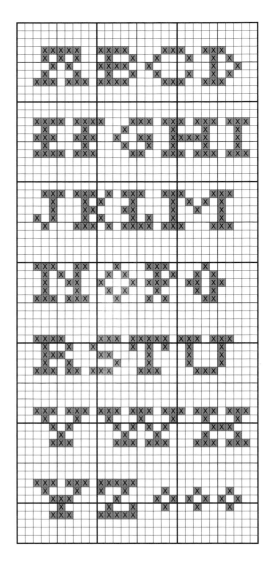

HONEYSUCKLE RING PILLOW KEY

Stranded cotton (floss)

DMC	ANCHOR		DMC	ANCHOR	
502	244		712	2	Anchor Multicolour 1335
503	240		729	306	Mill Hill Petite glass beads 40123
561	246		3731	54	
564	158		3733	50	Position of lettering (or tied-on wedding rings)
676	301		3813	1070	

Honeysuckle and Hardanger Hearts

*T*his beautiful design has a wealth of stitches for you to try – cross stitch, of course, but also bullion
stitches, Kloster blocks, needleweaving, wrapped bars, dove's eyes, spider's webs, woven leaves and
woven fans – all combined to produce a truly stunning picture.

Stitch count
108 x 120

Design size
19.5 x 21.75cm
(7¾ x 8½in)

YOU WILL NEED

33 x 36cm (13 x 14in)
Cashel linen 28-count,
shade 224 buttermilk

Tapestry needles sizes
24 and 22

Beading needle or size
10 sharp

Stranded cotton (floss)
as listed in chart key

Perlé cotton No 8 ecru

Perlé cotton No 12 ecru

Mill Hill Petite glass
beads, pearl (40123)

1 Fold the fabric in four and mark the folds with tacking (basting) stitches. Work the design from the centre of the fabric and the centre of the chart overleaf. Using a loop start (see page 8) work the cross stitch over two fabric threads, using two strands of stranded cotton (floss) for cross stitch and one for backstitch.

2 To work the Kloster blocks, use one strand of perlé cotton No 8 and an away waste knot and refer to the technique panel on page 74. When all blocks are complete and checked, cut the fabric threads as indicated on the chart. (The small chart gives an example of which threads can be cut.)

3 Decorate the remaining threads with wrapped bars and needleweaving using one strand of perlé cotton No 12 – see technique panel, right. Add the filling stitches (bullion stitches, dove's eye stitch, corner dove's eye, spider's web stitch, woven leaves and woven fans) whilst working the wrapped bars and needleweaving – refer to the chart and Stitch Library for instructions.

4 Use a beading needle and a half cross stitch to add the glass beads as shown on the chart.

5 When stitching is complete, check for missed stitches, remove tacking (basting) and then mount and frame as a picture (see page 116).

WORKING WRAPPED BARS AND NEEDLEWEAVING
Wrapped bars and needleweaving are techniques used to decorate threads that remain after cutting. They can be worked alone or with other stitches such as spider's web.

WRAPPED BARS

● Use one strand of perlé No 12 and start by anchoring the thread under adjacent Kloster blocks at the back and begin wrapping from a cut area.

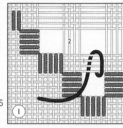

● Wind the thread round and round the four threads, then travel to the next group of threads and repeat.

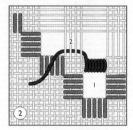

NEEDLEWEAVING

● Use one strand of perlé 12 and start by anchoring the thread as for wrapped bars. Begin from a cut area, bringing the needle up through a void and weaving the needle under and over pairs of threads in a plaited effect.

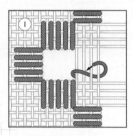

● After completing one bar, weave the next one at right angles to it, working around the design, taking care not to run threads across the back of the cut areas. Needleweaving should not alter the shape of the bar, which should stay flat and straight.

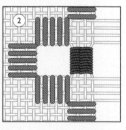

See Stitch Library pages 112 and 113 for corner needleweaving and woven leaves.

Tip
If you do cut a thread unintentionally – don't panic! Just remove the thread and take a fabric thread from the edge of the material and darn it in and out so that it replaces the cut thread.

See thread cutting diagram below

Spider's web in perlé 12 ecru

Woven fan in perlé 12 ecru

Dove's eye in perlé 12 ecru

Needleweaving in perlé 12 ecru

Corner dove's eye in perlé 12 ecru

Woven leaves in perlé 12 ecru

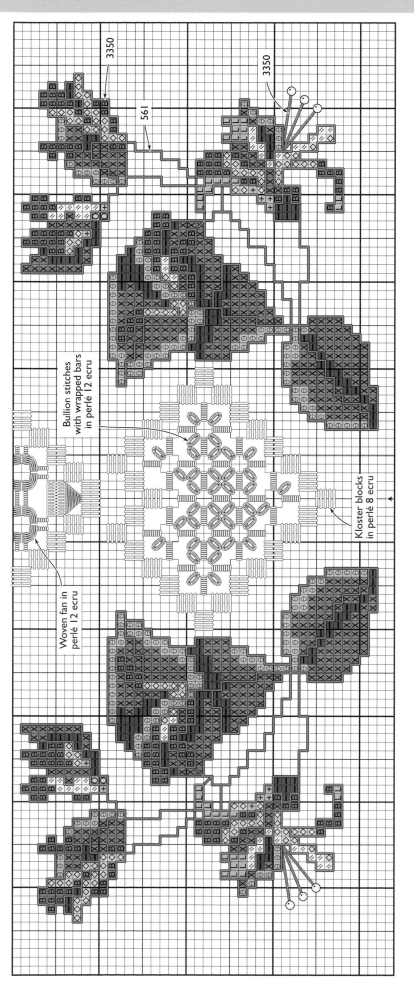

Bullion stitches
with wrapped bars
in perlé 12 ecru

Woven fan in
perlé 12 ecru

Kloster blocks
in perlé 8 ecru

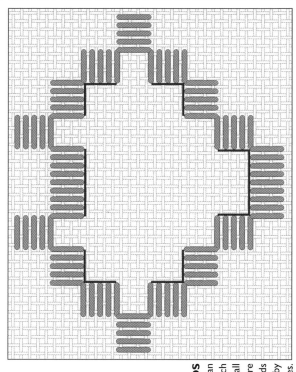

⊗ Mill Hill Petite glass beads pearl 40123

All Kloster blocks in
Perlé cotton 8 ecru
All filling stitches in
Perlé cotton 12 ecru

CUTTING THREADS
This chart gives an example of which threads to cut after all Kloster blocks are completed. Cut threads only where indicated by the red lines.

HONEYSUCKLE AND HARDANGER HEARTS KEY
Stranded cotton (floss)

DMC	ANCHOR		DMC	ANCHOR
502	244		729	306
503	240		3350	29
561	246		3731	54
564	158		3733	50
676	301		3813	1070
712	2			

79

Space-Dyed Spot Motifs

S pot motif samplers are very inspirational as they are a collection of favourite patterns stitched for their own sake and often quite random in character. Originally stitched during the 17th century in England, these types of samplers were partly a record of stitches and patterns and also used as appliqué. Designs were stitched in a haphazard way on a piece of fabric and kept until needed. In some cases, individual motifs would be cut out and applied to a garment or piece of furnishing.

The Stuart silk flower sampler featured in this chapter (so called because I had some copies of old engravings of flowers from the Stuart period and thought they were just perfect for this project) uses space-dyed threads on linen to achieve an antique appearance. Space-dyed threads are now readily available from many manufacturers and may be made from silk, rayon and cotton. These threads are not randomly dyed but have patterns of colour, making it possible to decide where you want a particular shade. If you cannot find the exact version used in this project try something else.

The sampler shown here has been made up as a framed picture but could be completed as a gorgeous cushion instead. Spot motifs are also perfect for using on smaller projects – the individual motifs can feature in simple gift cards, as used here, or added to trinket pots, pincushion bases or even table linen.

HONEYSUCKLE GIFT CARD

Stitch count 37 x 34

Design size 7 x 6cm (2¾ x 2½in)

This honeysuckle motif from the chart on page 85 was stitched over one block of 14-count cream Aida using two strands of a combination of 760 and 761 stranded cotton (floss) for cross stitch and one strand for backstitch. The design was cut out and frayed to within one square of the stitching and mounted on to handmade paper and a plain white card.

Stuart Silk Flower Sampler

This beautiful sampler (shown on page 81) was worked on linen to create a classic appearance but could be worked over one block of a 14-count Aida instead. Space-dyed threads are such fun to work with as you can never be quite sure what effect will be created (see technique panel for advice).

Stitch count
110 x 90

Design size
20 x 16.5cm (8 x 6½in)

YOU WILL NEED

33 x 30.5cm (13 x 12in) Cashel 28-count linen, shade 222

Tapestry needle size 26

Stranded cotton (floss) as listed in chart key

Pearsall's silk threads as in key (see Suppliers)

Caron Waterlilies as in key (see Suppliers)

1 Fold the fabric in four and mark the folds with tacking (basting) stitches. For this project, always start with an away waste knot (page 8) so that the variegated colour order isn't disrupted.

2 Work the design from the chart on pages 84 and 85, starting at the centre of the fabric. Work over two fabric threads (or one block if on Aida), using two strands of all threads for cross stitch and three-quarter cross stitch and one strand for backstitch. When cross stitching with space-dyed threads, always complete each cross and do not form in two journeys.

3 When all the stitching is complete, remove any tacking (basting) and make up as a picture with a padded mount (see page 116).

USING SPACE-DYED THREADS

There are many beautiful space-dyed threads available to stitchers today and the Caron Waterlilies range used in this spot sampler are simply delicious. The texture of the pure silk thread is wonderful and adds a subtle shimmer and sheen to your work.

● Look at the skein and cut the thread so that you can see where colours start and finish. Use a length of thread *only* whilst the colours are suiting the project. Avoid the cross stitcher's lament, 'I will waste thread' and do not use the whole thread if it's not appropriate.

● When combining stranded cottons with space-dyed threads, compare the colours carefully along the length of the thread to check that the shades tone successfully.

● When threading the needle, check that the colour you intend to use is near the away waste knot.

● Always complete each cross stitch – do not form in two journeys or the colour sequence will be interrupted.

● Manufacturers take great care to ensure that their threads are colourfast but some space-dyed threads can be suspect. Read the label on the threads and take sensible precautions if you are likely to wash the project. If in any doubt, lay the stitching right side down on a clean, flat surface and using a damp white tissue, press the threads firmly, particularly red shades. If there is even a trace of colour on the tissue, do not wash the project!

GRAPE GIFT CARD

Stitch count *29 x 24*

Design size *5 x 4.5cm (2 x 1¾in)*

This simple grape motif from the chart on page 85 was stitched over two threads of Cashel 28-count linen, shade 770 (or use a 14-count Aida), using two strands of stranded cotton (floss) for cross stitch and one for backstitch. It was mounted on a handmade blue card and trimmed with pretty pastel ribbon.

STRAWBERRY PICTURE

Stitch count 43 x 36

Design size 8 x 6.5cm (3 x 2½in)

This pretty strawberry design from the main chart was stitched over two threads of Cashel 28-count linen shade 633 (or use a 14-count Aida), using two strands of stranded cotton (floss) for cross stitch and one for backstitch. It was stretched and mounted in a gold-coloured frame.

Tip

If you prefer not to use variegated threads, for a different look you could choose a stranded cotton or silk colour to blend with the design, as in the honeysuckle gift card on page 80.

PINK ROSE CARD

Stitch count 34 x 39

Design size 6 x 7cm (2½ x 2¾in)

This card was stitched from the main chart over two threads of antique white 28-count Cashel linen (or use a 14-count Aida), using two strands of stranded cotton (floss) for cross stitch and one for backstitch. The design was cut out to within ten threads of the stitching, frayed, trimmed and attached to a piece of handmade paper and plain white card covered in dolls' house wallpaper.

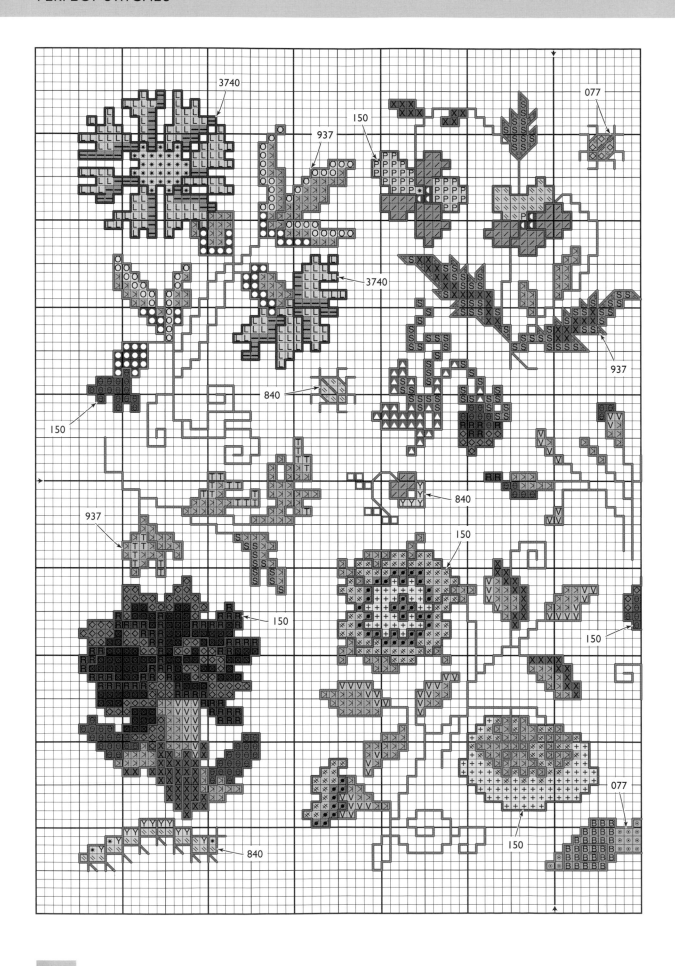

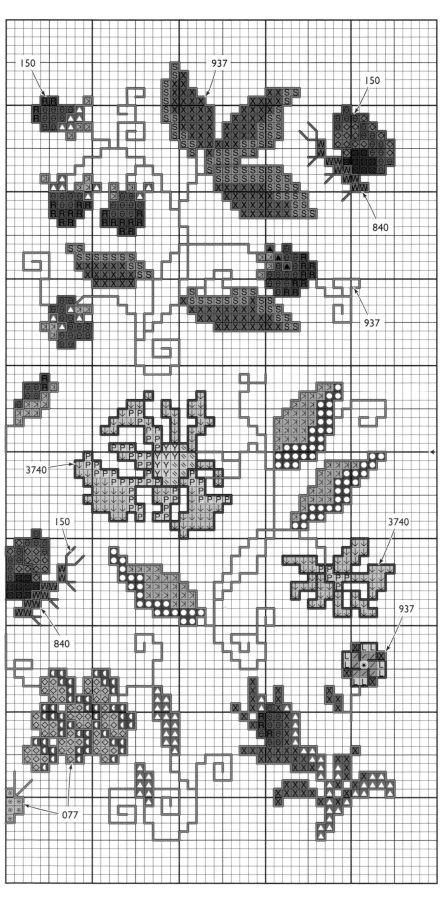

STUART SILK FLOWER SAMPLER KEY
Stranded cotton (floss)

	DMC	ANCHOR		DMC	ANCHOR
	150	29		676	301
	223	10		840	371
	224	1021		937	269
	225	271		3041	1018
	367	245		3052	265
	503	240		3347	239
	520	382		3350	29
	522	238		3731	54
	524	259		3740	972

Pearsall's Silk

	077
	134
	159
	164
	197
	240

Caron Waterlilies

	Cedar
	Mountain Meadow
	Olive
	Hyacinth
	Pebbles
	African Sunset

Heirloom Band Samplers

Many poems and embroidery books over the centuries have praised the wonderful work achieved with needle and thread. As early as 1624 in England, *A Scholehouse for the Needle* was a popular book for its spot motifs of birds, flowers and fishes. This band sampler is my praise to the glories of the needle, and shows how to create your own 'heirloom band sampler'. This sampler (and the Sulgrave Sampler, a slightly more complicated one that follows) needs to be stitched on an evenweave fabric because many of the stitches cannot be worked on Aida.

Originally, band samplers were made from long, thin strips of linen and were not intended to be decorative but to be points of reference or *aides-mémoire* to stitchers. Patterns were copied and stitches practised and when not in use, the sampler would be carefully rolled up and put safe in a drawer. The 'bands' of stitching could feature dozens of stitches, including cross stitch, herringbone stitch, Algerian eye, hollie-point and queen stitch. Antique band samplers from the 17th century are very collectable and can cost thousands of pounds. This is an opportunity to work your own antique-style sampler for a fraction of the cost!

The patterns and motifs in band samplers can be used alone or re-combined to make new designs, or worked on other fabrics. As you will see in this chapter, parts of the Needle's Prayse chart have been used to create three additional projects – a pretty Violet purse, a small Alphabet sampler and a Deer gift card, shown here.

DEER GIFT CARD

Stitch count 21 x 22

Design size 4 x 4cm (1½ x 1½in)

This little card was cross stitched on 16-count Aida using two strands of stranded cotton (floss). The work was then frayed to within four blocks of the stitching and mounted as a simple patch on a card. See page 118 for card making.

The Needle's Prayse Band Sampler

Stitch count

78 x 394

Design size

14 x 71.5cm

(5½ x 28in)

YOU WILL NEED

30.5 x 84cm

(12 x 33in) Zweigart
Cashel unbleached
28-count linen

Tapestry needles sizes
26 and 22

Stranded cottons (floss)
as listed in chart key

Perlé cotton No 8 ecru

Perlé cotton No 12
ecru

Madeira Gold No 15
shade 22

*T*his band sampler (shown on previous page) is in praise of the beautiful effects that can be achieved just with a needle and thread. It is made up of forty bands, containing a satisfying number of different stitches, combined with some pulled thread work – it's bound to become an heirloom you'll treasure.

1 It is important to prepare the linen for work and mark guidelines, see page 7. Start stitching in the middle of the fabric to ensure adequate space for finishing, working the design from the centre of the chart, completing one of the cross stitch bands first (Band 21) to help to 'get your eye in' before attempting any of the other decorative stitches.

2 Work a line of tacking (basting) stitches down each side of the fabric starting at the end of the completed cross stitch band. This will help to place the next stitches and act as a warning if you have miscounted. All the bands are worked in cross stitch except those detailed below. Page numbers refer to diagrams in the Stitch Library or other detailed instructions.

Generally, use two strands of stranded cotton (floss) for the full and three-quarter cross stitches, double cross stitch, Algerian eye, French knots, half eyelets, pseudo couching, satin stitch, half Rhodes stitch and Queen stitch. Work Holbein stitch, backstitch and hemstitching with one strand.

3 When the band sampler is complete, either hemstitch the edges as shown on page 20 or mount and frame as a picture (see page 116) or make up as a bell pull (see page 117).

BAND 1 Assorted motifs including cross stitch, hemstitch square, needleweaving, satin stitch, Rhodes stitch and queen stitch
Hemstitch Square – Refer to the technique panel overleaf for working a hemstitch square. Use one strand of perlé 12 for hemstitch around the cutwork area, referring to the chart.
Needleweaving – Once the threads have been cut and tacked (basted) out of the way,

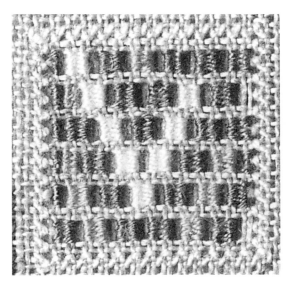

needleweave the remaining vertical threads in pairs in 712, 327 and 729 (see technique panel overleaf). When needleweaving is complete use two strands of 712 stranded cotton (floss) to work satin stitch around the edge between the cutwork and the hemstitch. Once completed, cut away the loose threads.
Queen stitch – Use two strands of 3777 and see diagrams on page 111.

BANDS 2 & 9 Rice stitch
Work the rice stitch (page 111) in two colours, the large cross over four threads in two strands of stranded cotton (floss) and the small stitches in one strand of Madeira gold metallic.

BANDS 4, 12, 17, 22 & 27 Hemstitch, zigzag hemstitch, somersault stitch, ladder hemstitch and tied hemstitch
Work the various hemstitch bands (see Stitch Library page 114). Remove the number of threads stated on the chart, then hemstitch the remaining verticals using ecru perlé cotton No 12 – completing Band 4 as zigzag hemstitch,

SQUARE ALPHABET SAMPLER

Stitch count 78 x 75

Design size 14 x 14cm (5½ x 5½in)

This little sampler uses motifs from the main chart and was stitched on 16-count Aida instead of linen, using two strands of stranded cotton (floss). On the version shown, I replaced the cream colour with an Anchor Multicolour stranded cotton (floss) shade 1335 with great success.

Band 12 as somersault stitch, Bands 17 and 22 as ladder hemstitch and Band 27 as tied hemstitch. The picture details below show bands 11, 12 and 13 with half eyelets and somersault stitch, and below that Bands 26, 27 and 28 with half eyelets and tied hemstitch.

stitches right to left on the right side. Pass the needle to the back and finish off (see detail photo below, which also shows Band 5).

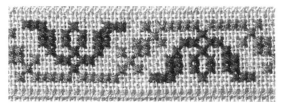

BANDS 7, 18, 20 & 32 Double cross stitch
See page 107 and chart for colours.

BANDS 11, 13, 26 & 28 Half eyelets
See page 108 and chart for colours.

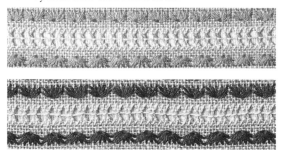

BAND 6 Pseudo couching
Work a line of half cross stitches in 315 from left to right and then thread the needle through these

BANDS 16, 23, 25 & 38 Holbein stitch and three-quarter cross stitch
See pages 110 and 107 and chart for colours.

BAND 29 Cross stitch, queen stitch and mini-band

Queen stitch – Use two strands of 3051.

Mini-band – This features various repeated stitches – see key below. Refer to the picture detail here and the Stitch Library for working the stitches.

STITCHES KEY
① Double cross stitch
② Algerian eyes
③ Half eyelets
④ Half Rhodes stitch with bar & satin stitch
⑤ Pseudo couching

BAND 33 Cross stitch, backstitch and Hardanger embroidery

See technique panels on page 74 and 77 for working Kloster blocks and needleweaving.

WORKING A HEMSTITCH SQUARE

A hemstitched square (or rectangle) is an attractive design to include in any sampler and can be any size you choose (see the smaller one in the Sulgrave Sampler on page 98).

● Referring to the chart and counting the area carefully, use one strand of perlé cotton No 12 and work basic hemstitch around the cutwork area.

● Once the hemstitching is complete, count to the centre of the hemmed area and carefully cut alternate pairs of horizontal threads across the square.

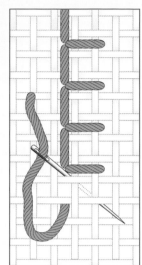

● Carefully unravel the cut threads from the middle to the hemstitched edge, leaving a two-thread border at the sides for satin stitch later. On the back of the work, loosely tack (baste) these threads out of the way.

● Needleweave the remaining vertical threads in pairs in a similar fashion to that shown in the technique panel on page 77 but over only two threads.

● When the needleweaving is complete, use two strands of the stranded cotton (floss) colour given on the chart to work straight satin stitch around the edge between the cutwork and the hemstitch. Once completed, cut away the loose threads.

VIOLET PURSE

Stitch count 78 x 35

Design size 15.25 x 7cm (6 x 2¾in)

This purse features bands from the main chart. It was cross stitched over two threads of 27-count Zweigart Meran shade 440 using two strands of stranded cotton (floss). See page 119 for making up.

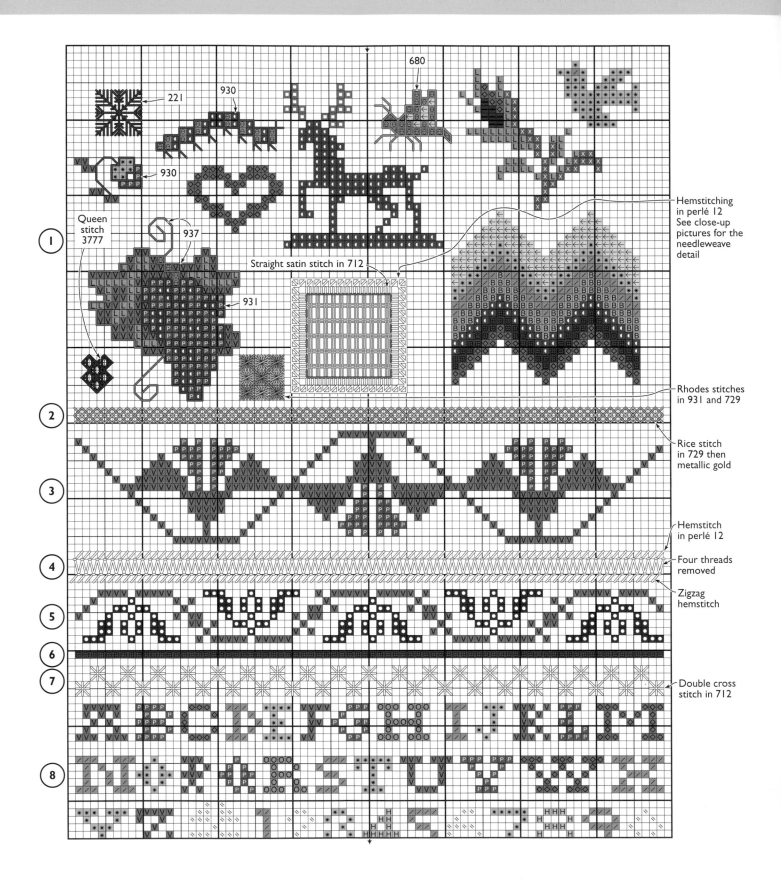

① Queen stitch 3777
221
930
930
937
931
680
Straight satin stitch in 712

Hemstitching in perlé 12 See close-up pictures for the needleweave detail

Rhodes stitches in 931 and 729

② Rice stitch in 729 then metallic gold

③

④ Hemstitch in perlé 12
Four threads removed
Zigzag hemstitch

⑤

⑥

⑦ Double cross stitch in 712

⑧

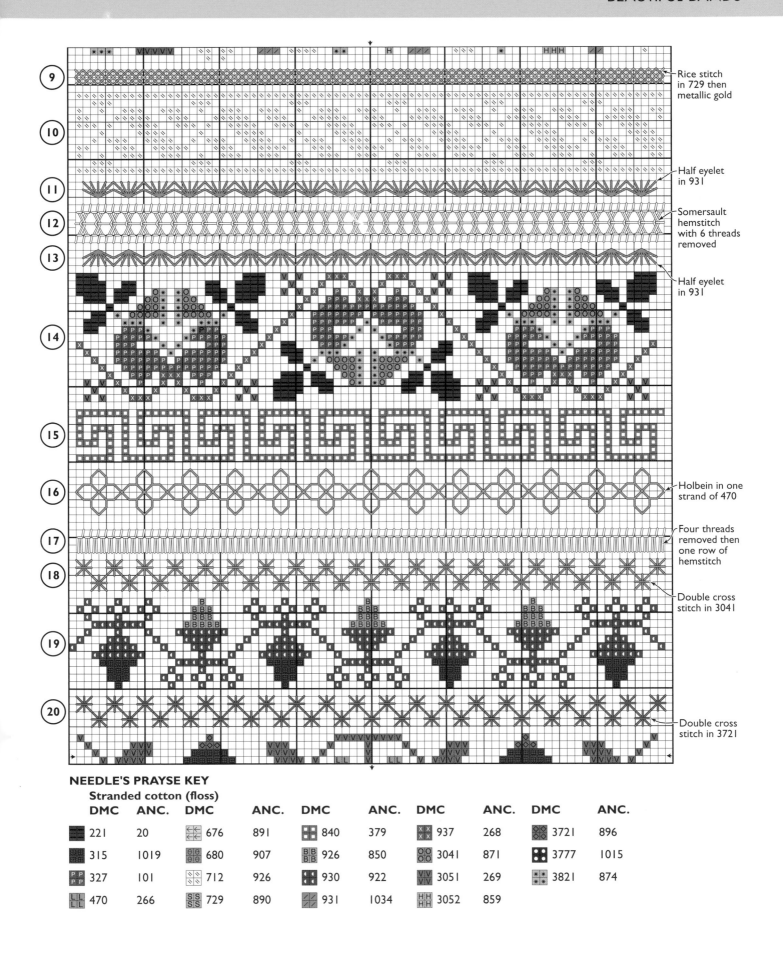

Rice stitch in 729 then metallic gold

Half eyelet in 931

Somersault hemstitch with 6 threads removed

Half eyelet in 931

Holbein in one strand of 470

Four threads removed then one row of hemstitch

Double cross stitch in 3041

Double cross stitch in 3721

NEEDLE'S PRAYSE KEY
Stranded cotton (floss)

DMC	ANC.	DMC	ANC.	DMC	ANC.	DMC	ANC.	DMC	ANC.
221	20	676	891	840	379	937	268	3721	896
315	1019	680	907	926	850	3041	871	3777	1015
327	101	712	926	930	922	3051	269	3821	874
470	266	729	890	931	1034	3052	859		

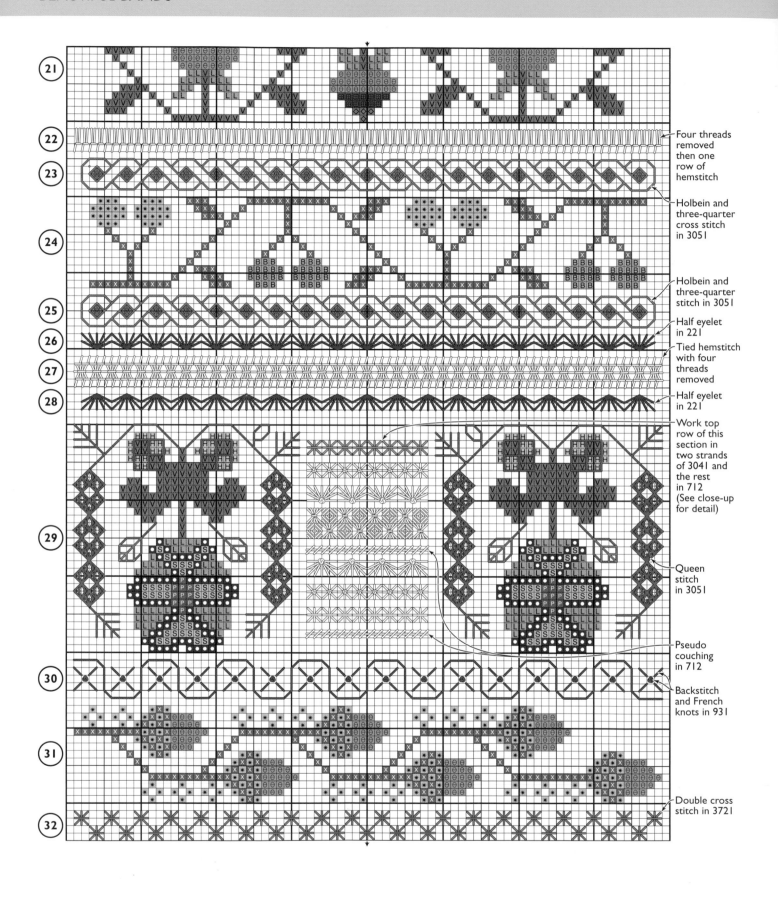

21

22 — Four threads removed then one row of hemstitch

23 — Holbein and three-quarter cross stitch in 3051

24

25 — Holbein and three-quarter stitch in 3051

26 — Half eyelet in 221

27 — Tied hemstitch with four threads removed

28 — Half eyelet in 221

29 — Work top row of this section in two strands of 3041 and the rest in 712 (See close-up for detail)

Queen stitch in 3051

Pseudo couching in 712

30 — Backstitch and French knots in 931

31

32 — Double cross stitch in 3721

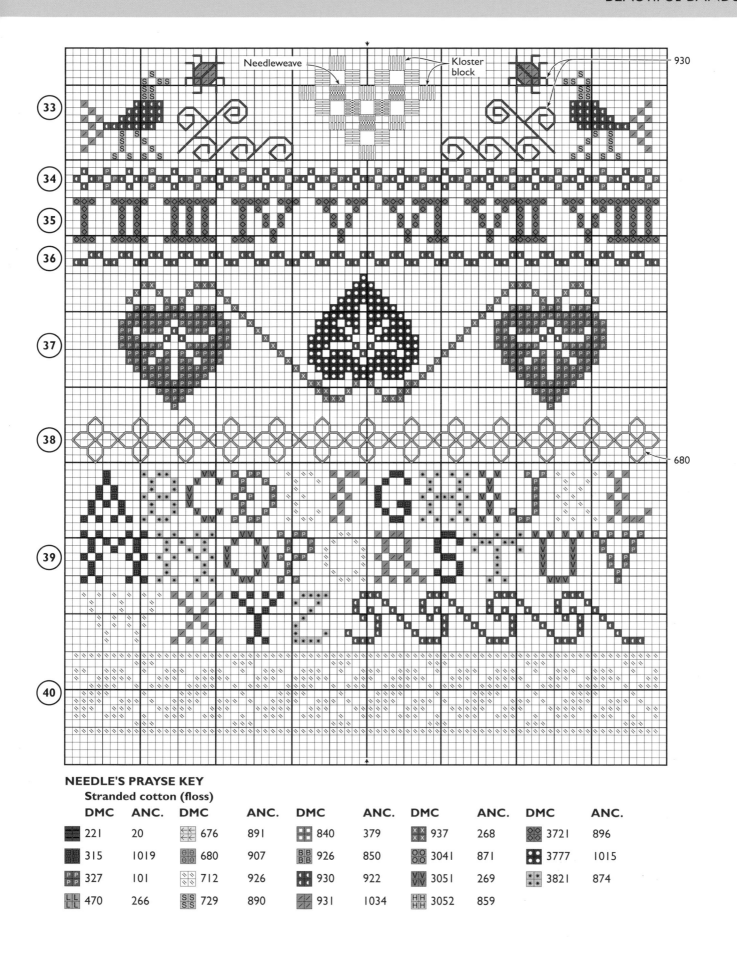

NEEDLE'S PRAYSE KEY
Stranded cotton (floss)

DMC	ANC.	DMC	ANC.	DMC	ANC.	DMC	ANC.	DMC	ANC.
221	20	676	891	840	379	937	268	3721	896
315	1019	680	907	926	850	3041	871	3777	1015
327	101	712	926	930	922	3051	269	3821	874
470	266	729	890	931	1034	3052	859		

Band Inspirations

Samplers have a long and interesting history spanning many centuries. The word sampler or exampler is thought to be derived from the French *éxamplair*, meaning a kind of model or pattern to copy from or imitate.

Samplers today are often regarded as purely decorative objects associated with interor design but historically they provided an invaluable record of stitches and a library of patterns. Apart from being works of reference, samplers were also stitched to depict family trees, whilst others commemorated life events such as weddings or births. Embroiderers would be inspired by what they saw around them and created patterns and motifs accordingly.

This is how the Sulgrave sampler came to be, inspired by Sulgrave Manor, near Banbury, England, the ancestral home of United States President, George Washington. I have spent many a happy hour in this beautiful house and out in the gorgeous garden and I was simply inspired to create this sampler. I made notes and sketches whilst being 'Artist in Residence' and it grew from there. The sampler could have been even longer because there is so much inspirational material at Sulgrave Manor.

The Sulgrave sampler has many lovely spot motifs and interesting bands to feature in smaller projects and I have included two ideas in this chapter – a handy stitcher's etui that makes a useful case for many small needlework items and a pretty Hardanger needlecase.

HARDANGER NEEDLECASE

Stitch count 34 x 32

Design size 6 x 5.8cm (2½ x 2¼in)

This was stitched over two fabric threads on a 15 x 13cm (6 x 5in) piece of 28-count unbleached linen, using a flower motif from the Sulgrave sampler chart (Band 15) and a Hardanger motif – the perfect chance to design your own. The linen was folded in two, the fold marked with tacking (basting) stitches and the designs worked on one half. A folded hem was worked with hem-stitching (see page 20) and a lining of handkerchief linen stitched into place from the inside in matching thread, with a piece of flannel added for the needle pages.

The Sulgrave Sampler

This sampler is a little more complicated than the Needle's Prayse but is sure to become an heirloom to be proud of. It must be stitched on evenweave fabric because many of the stitches cannot be worked on Aida. It could be hemstitched like the Needle's Prayse or made in to a bell pull as shown on page 97.

Stitch count
79 x 397

Design size
14.3 x 72cm
(5⅝ x 28¼in)

YOU WILL NEED

*36 x 91cm (14 x 38in)
Cashel linen 28-count,
unbleached shade 55*

*Tapestry needles sizes
24 and 22*

*Beading needle or size
10 sharp*

*Stranded cottons (floss)
as listed in chart key*

Perlé cotton No 8 ecru

Perlé cotton No 12 ecru

*Kreinik metallic Ombre
1500*

*Madeira Gold No 15
shade 22*

*Mill Hill Antique glass
beads as listed in key*

*Small amount of
wadding (batting)*

1 It is important to prepare the linen for work and mark guidelines, see page 7. Start stitching over two fabric threads, in the middle of the fabric to ensure adequate space for finishing, working the design from the centre of the chart, completing one of the cross stitch bands first (Band 18) to help to 'get your eye in' before attempting any of the other decorative stitches.

2 Work a line of tacking (basting) stitches down each side of the fabric starting at the end of the completed cross stitch band (at the edges of the butterflies). This will help to place the next stitches and act as a warning if you have miscounted. All the bands are worked in cross stitch except those detailed below. Refer to the Stitch Library for working the stitches.

Use two strands of stranded cotton (floss) for full, three-quarter and double cross stitches, Algerian eyes, French knots, satin stitch, half Rhodes stitch, bullion stitch, lazy daisy stitch and buttonhole wheels. Work backstitches, Holbein (double running) stitch and half eyelets in one strand.

Work Kloster blocks in one strand of ecru perlé cotton No 8. Work the needleweaving and hemstitch bands with one strand of ecru perlé cotton No 12, or as stated on the chart. Use a beading needle to attach beads, with one strand of cream thread and a half cross stitch.

3 When the band sampler is complete, either hemstitch the edges as described on page 20 or make up as a bell pull (see page 117).

BAND 1 Assorted motifs including cross stitch, hemstitch square with wrapped bars and dove's eye, needlelace flower and hollie-point acorn

Hemstitch Square – Refer to working a hemstitch square in the technique panel on page 90 (but cutting vertical *and* horizontal threads here). Using two strands of 842, work the hem-

stitch around the cutwork area shown on the chart. Cut the horizontal and vertical threads, snipping alternate sets of two threads across the square. Unravel the cut threads leaving a two-thread border at the sides and loosely tack (baste) these threads out of the way.

Wrapped bars and dove's eye – Wrap the remaining threads in pairs (see technique panel page 77), adding a dove's eye (page 113) as you proceed using one strand of 842. When this is complete use two strands of stranded cotton (floss) to work straight satin stitch in 842 around the edge between the cutwork and hemstitch. Once the square is complete, cut away the loose threads.

Hollie-point acorns – Work the cross-stitch section of the acorns and outline the acorn cup using one strand of 840. Work the hollie-point (page 110) starting from the top of the acorn cup. Before completing the last row slip a tiny amount of wadding (batting) or fleece inside the pocket that has been formed.

STITCHER'S ETUI

Stitch count 62 x 37 (front flap only)   Design size 11.25 x 6.75cm (4½ x 2¾in)

This little case was stitched over two fabric threads on a 28 x 33cm (11 x 13in) piece of 28-count unbleached linen, using the house from Band 18 on the front flap and the flower border (Band 27) under the flap. Fold the linen in three and work tacking (basting) lines along the folds. Work the house on one third and the flower border at the other end of the fabric but upside-down so that when made up it will be in the correct position. Work two rows of four-sided stitch along the folds to create hinges. Make up as shown on page 119. You could choose further motifs from the chart and work them on the back of the case.

BAND 2 Rice stitch

Work rice stitch (page 111) in two colours: the large cross over four threads in two strands 930 stranded cotton (floss) and the small stitches in one strand of Madeira gold metallic.

BANDS 4, 7, 11, 13, 20 & 28
Couching, diamond hemstitch, hemstitch, somersault stitch and double row hemstitch
Couch one strand of Kreinik Ombre in position with one strand of stranded cotton (floss) 221. Work the hemstitch bands (see Stitch Library page 114), removing the number of threads as stated on the chart, then hemstitch the remain-

ing verticals as on the chart. For Band 4, add the beads as a final row. For Band 7, remove eight threads and hemstitch in two strands of 842, then work beaded somersault stitch (page 115) in one strand of 842.

BANDS 6, 8, 19, 21 & 26 Half eyelets
Work half eyelets over four threads in one strand of the colour given on the chart. Band 21 has the addition of pearl beads.

BAND 10 Herringbone stitch
Work the herringbone stitch (page 115) using two strands of 3041.

BANDS 14, 16 & 30 Double cross stitch with diagonal satin stitch, Algerian eyes and half Rhodes stitch with bar

Work double cross stitch in the colours given on the chart over four threads, alternately with diagonal satin stitch in Band 14, Algerian eyes in Band 16 and half Rhodes stitch in Band 30.

BAND 17 Cross stitch and Hardanger

Work the band in cross stitch and add the Hardanger, needleweaving and dove's eye stitch in the threads given on the chart. See technique panels on pages 74 and 77 for working Kloster blocks and needleweaving.

BAND 23 Bullion stitch, French knots, beads

First backstitch outline the row as shown on the chart. Then, working at random, add French knots and lilac beads.

BANDS 24 & 33 Four-sided stitch

Work four-sided stitch over four threads in 712.

BAND 27 Flower border motif

Work in cross stitch, backstitch, French knots, buttonhole wheels, lazy daisy stitch and bullion stitch (see stitching detail and technique panel page 101 for working these last three stitches).

BAND 31 Cross stitch, Holbein stitch, bullion stitches and beads

Use cross stitch and Holbein stitch to create the flower motifs, then add bullion stitches and lilac beads as shown below.

BAND 34 Algerian eyes

Work Algerian eyes with two strands of 712.

WORKING BUTTONHOLE WHEELS, LAZY DAISY STITCH AND BULLION STITCH

These three stitches form parts of the flower garden in Band 27 and are useful stitches for creating interest and three-dimensional texture in a design.

BUTTONHOLE WHEELS

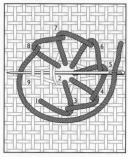

These are worked like buttonhole stitches but in a circle. Bring the needle up at 1 and down at 2 (in the centre) forming a loop. Come up at 3 and down at 2, anchoring the first loop and creating a second. Come up at 4 and down at 2 again, anchoring the second loop and creating a third, and so on around the circle.

LAZY DAISY STITCH

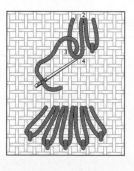

Bring the needle to the front at 1 and down at 2 forming a loop. Anchor the loop by bringing the needle up at 3 (inside loop) and down at 4 (outside). Stitches can be different lengths and angles.

BULLION STITCH

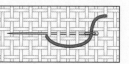

This stitch is formed by working an incomplete backstitch, leaving the needle in the fabric. It is vital that the point of the needle exits from the hole where it started.

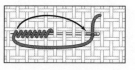

With the needle still in the fabric, wind the thread around the needle as many times as necessary to make the coil the length of the finished bar. Hold the needle and coil of thread firmly against the fabric, then gently but firmly pull the needle through the coil and fabric. Using a gold-plated needle makes this exercise much simpler. Turn the coil back on itself and push the needle through the fabric at the rear of the backstitch.

The bee in Band 27 is worked in alternate bullion stitches in 840 and 729, with back-stitch wings in 317 and a French knot in 840 at either end.

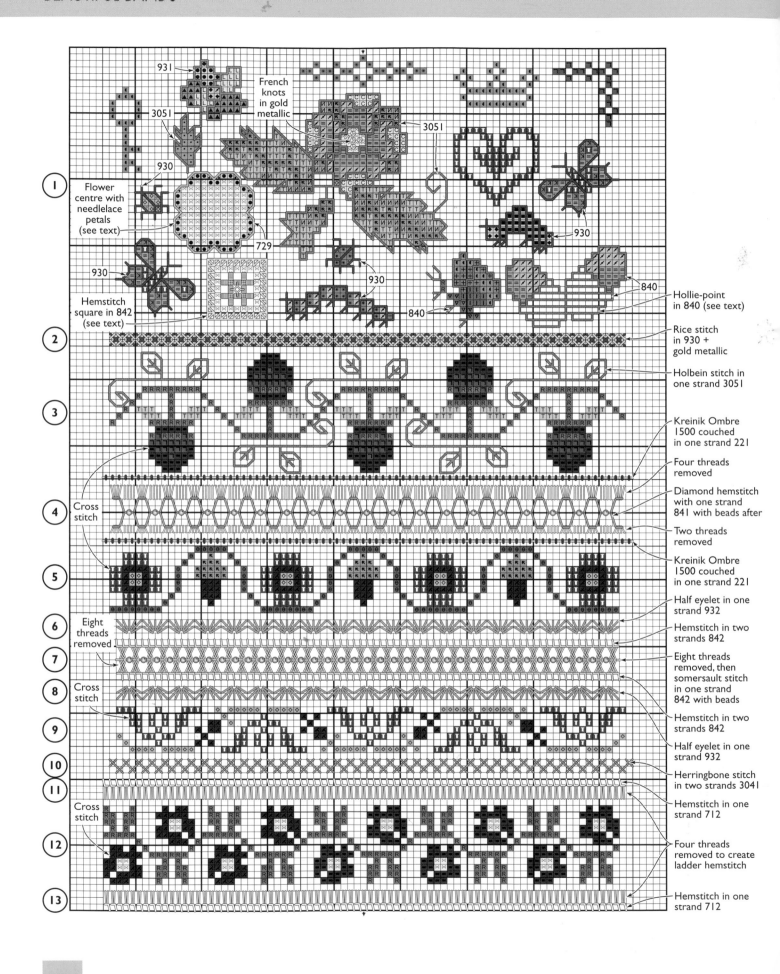

931
3051
930
Flower centre with needlelace petals (see text)
729
930
Hemstitch square in 842 (see text)
930
840
840

French knots in gold metallic
3051
930

Hollie-point in 840 (see text)

Rice stitch in 930 + gold metallic

Holbein stitch in one strand 3051

Kreinik Ombre 1500 couched in one strand 221

Four threads removed

Diamond hemstitch with one strand 841 with beads after

Two threads removed

Kreinik Ombre 1500 couched in one strand 221

Half eyelet in one strand 932

Hemstitch in two strands 842

Eight threads removed, then somersault stitch in one strand 842 with beads

Hemstitch in two strands 842

Half eyelet in one strand 932

Herringbone stitch in two strands 3041

Hemstitch in one strand 712

Four threads removed to create ladder hemstitch

Hemstitch in one strand 712

Cross stitch

Eight threads removed

Cross stitch

Cross stitch

1 2 3 4 5 6 7 8 9 10 11 12 13

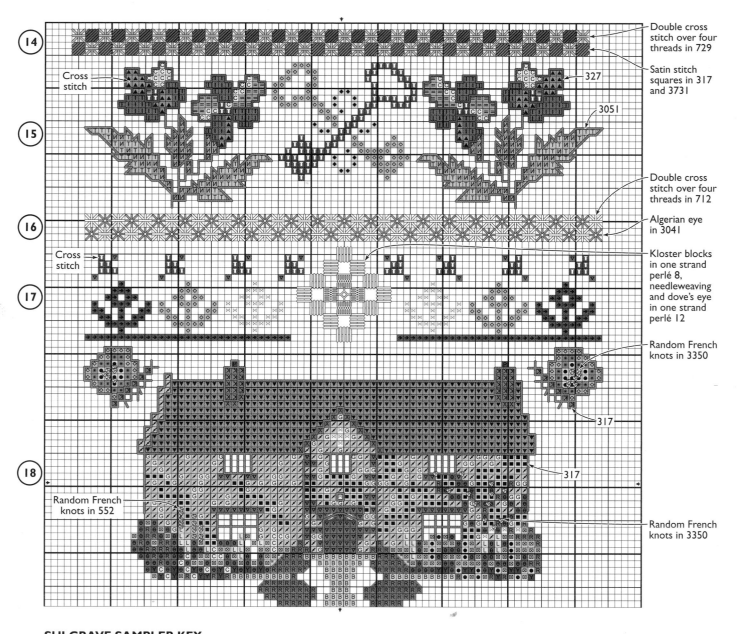

Double cross stitch over four threads in 729

Satin stitch squares in 317 and 3731

327

Cross stitch

3051

Double cross stitch over four threads in 712

Algerian eye in 3041

Cross stitch

Kloster blocks in one strand perlé 8, needleweaving and dove's eye in one strand perlé 12

Random French knots in 3350

317

317

Random French knots in 552

Random French knots in 3350

SULGRAVE SAMPLER KEY
Stranded cotton (floss)

	DMC	ANCHOR		DMC	ANCHOR		DMC	ANCHOR		DMC	ANCHOR
	221	1006		437	891		732	281		3041	1018
	223	10		470	256		738	279		3051	268
	301	13		522	261		733	880		3033	926
	317	878		552	88		840	944		3053	264
	327	94		611	898		842	387		3350	29
	367	245		676	301		926	208		3364	265
	413	382		677	386		930	1036		3731	29
	415	847		680	307		931	978		3740	972
	435	308		712	2		3012	365		3777	20
	436	363		729	306		3013	278		Madeira gold metallic	

French knots

	DMC	ANCHOR
	Madeira gold metallic	
	3350	29
	327	94
	552	88
	3041	1018
	3740	972

Mill Hill Glass Beads

	03023	lilac
	40479	pearl
	00283	blue

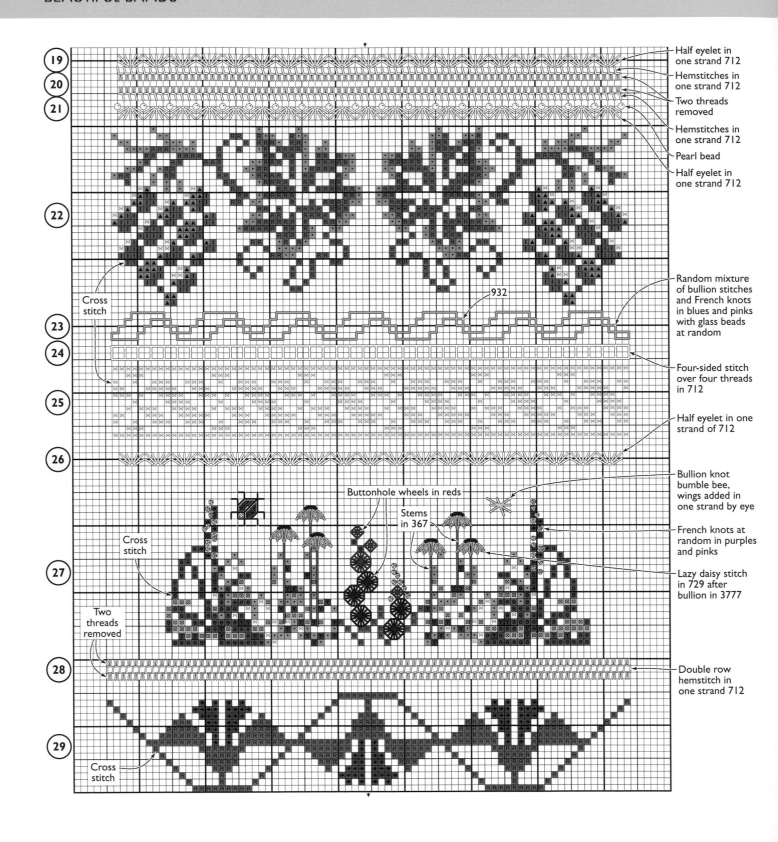

19 Half eyelet in one strand 712

20 Hemstitches in one strand 712

21 Two threads removed

Hemstitches in one strand 712

Pearl bead

Half eyelet in one strand 712

22 Cross stitch

932

Random mixture of bullion stitches and French knots in blues and pinks with glass beads at random

23

24 Four-sided stitch over four threads in 712

25

Half eyelet in one strand of 712

26

Bullion knot bumble bee, wings added in one strand by eye

Buttonhole wheels in reds

Stems in 367

French knots at random in purples and pinks

27 Cross stitch

Lazy daisy stitch in 729 after bullion in 3777

Two threads removed

28 Double row hemstitch in one strand 712

29 Cross stitch

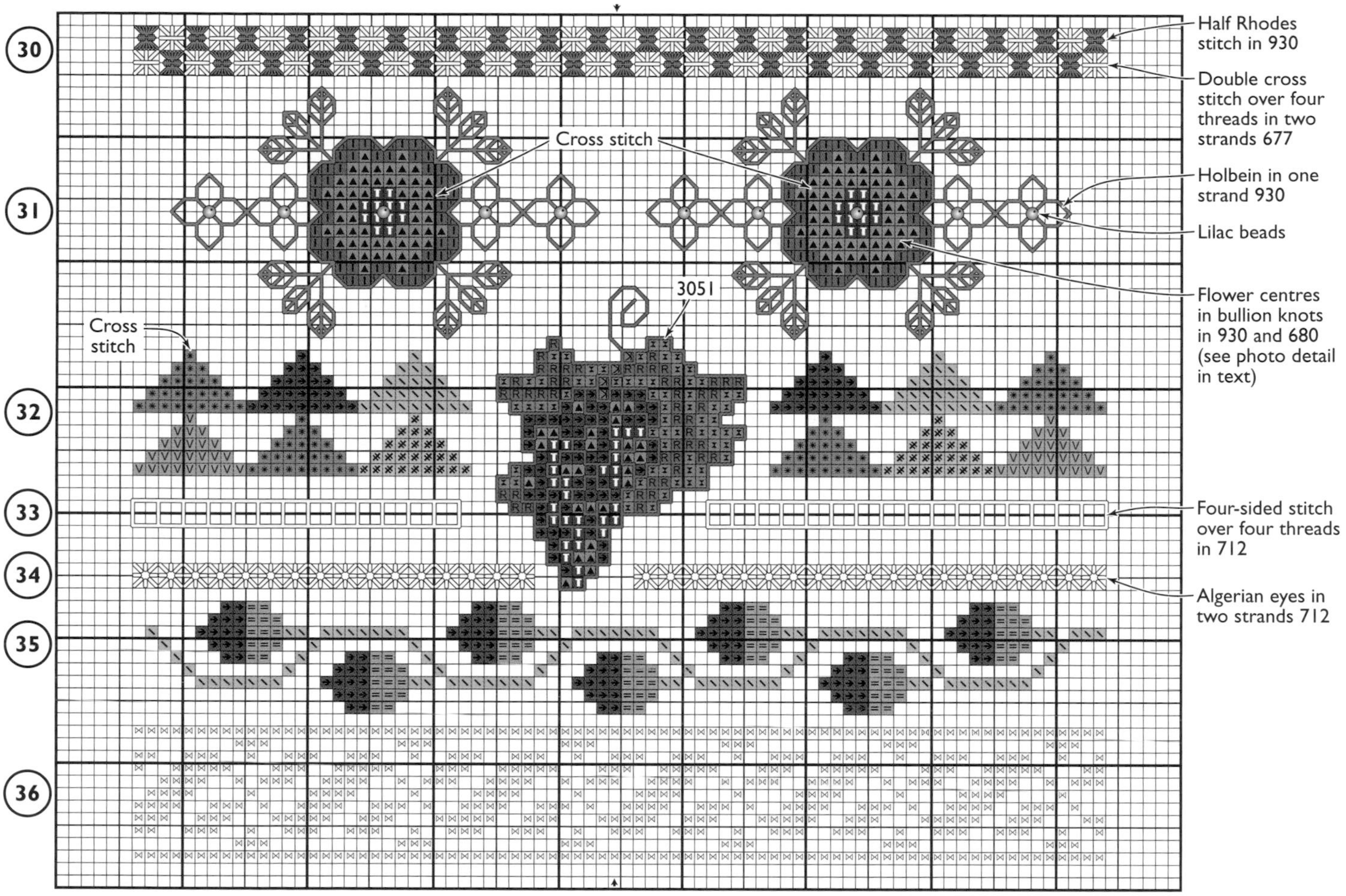

30
31
32
33
34
35
36
Half Rhodes stitch in 930
Double cross stitch over four threads in two strands 677
Cross stitch
Holbein in one strand 930
Lilac beads
Flower centres in bullion knots in 930 and 680 (see photo detail in text)
3051
Cross stitch
Four-sided stitch over four threads in 712
Algerian eyes in two strands 712

SULGRAVE SAMPLER KEY

Stranded cotton (floss)

DMC	ANCHOR	DMC	ANCHOR	DMC	ANCHOR	DMC	ANCHOR
221	1006	437	891	732	281	3041	1018
223	10	470	256	738	279	3051	268
301	13	522	261	733	880	3033	926
317	878	552	88	840	944	3053	264
327	94	611	898	842	387	3350	29
367	245	676	301	926	208	3364	265
413	382	677	386	930	1036	3731	29
415	847	680	307	931	978	3740	972
435	308	712	2	3012	365	3777	20
436	363	729	306	3013	278	Madeira gold metallic	

French knots

DMC	ANCHOR
Madeira gold metallic	
3350	29
327	94
552	88
3041	1018
3740	972

Mill Hill Glass Beads

03023 lilac
40479 pearl
00283 blue

Stitch Library

*T*he stitches used in this book are described here beginning with general stitches (alphabetically), followed by Hardanger stitches and hemstitches. In many cases the stitches may be worked on Aida, evenweave or canvas unless stated otherwise, although some pulled stitches are not as effective when worked on Aida. I find it very useful to have a large count (20-count) scrap of fabric at hand to practise any new stitches on before working them on a project. Some of the diagrams show the stitch worked over two or four fabric threads. Remember that when working a stitch, the construction will stay the same but the size and number of fabric threads used may alter. Always refer to the chart for the correct number of fabric threads involved. When constructing a stitch, remember which way you worked and keep all the stitches the same, clockwise or anticlockwise.

GENERAL STITCHES (alphabetical order)

ALGERIAN EYE

This pretty star-shaped stitch is a pulled stitch which means that when formed correctly holes are pulled in the fabric. It can be worked over two or four threads of evenweave and is more successful worked on evenweave than Aida.

1 Start to the left of a vertical thread and work from left to right around each stitch in an anticlockwise direction (or vice versa but keeping each stitch the same).

2 Always work the stitch by passing the needle down through the central hole, pulling quite firmly so that a small hole is formed in the centre. Take care that trailing threads do not cover this hole as you progress to the next stitch.

BACKSTITCH

Backstitch is used for outlining a design or part of a design, to add detail or emphasis, or for lettering. It is usually indicated on a chart by solid lines with the suggested shade indicated on the chart or key. It is added

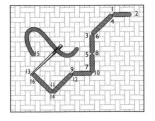

after the cross stitch has been completed, to prevent the backstitch line being broken by the cross stitches.

To work backstitch, follow the numbered sequence in the diagram, working the stitches over one block of Aida or over two threads of evenweave, unless stated otherwise on the chart. Avoid using long, loose stitches unless used for ship rigging, cat's whiskers and so on.

BULLION STITCH

This is a very versatile stitch which can be formed in straight bars or in curves, and which has been used in many of the samplers in the book.

1 The stitch is formed by working an incomplete backstitch, leaving the needle in the fabric. It is vital that the point of the needle exits from the hole where it started.

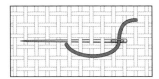

2 With the needle still in the fabric, wind the thread around the needle as many times as necessary to make the coil the length of the finished bar. Hold

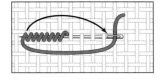

the needle and coil of thread firmly against the fabric, then gently pull the needle through the coil and fabric. Using a gold-plated needle makes this exercise much simpler. To finish the stitch turn the coil back on itself and push the needle through the fabric at the rear of the backstitch.

BUTTONHOLE WHEELS

These are worked like buttonhole stitches but in a circle. Bring the needle up at 1 and down at 2 (in the centre) forming a loop. Come up at 3 and down at 2, anchoring the first loop and creating a second. Come up at 4 and down at 2 again, anchoring the second loop and creating a third, and so on around the circle.

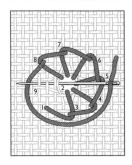

COUCHING

This is not a counted stitch as such but can be very effective, particularly on a band sampler. Couching is often worked with

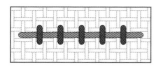

a metallic thread laid on the fabric, held down by small vertical stitches. Start by bringing the laid thread up through the fabric and laying it across the fabric. Using the couching thread, work small vertical stitches, as shown.

CROSS STITCH

This simple stitch is the key to counted embroidery. Cross stitches can be worked singly or in two journeys but you should always keep the top stitch facing the same direction. It does not matter which way it faces but it should be the same for the whole project.

Cross stitch on Aida

Cross stitch on Aida fabric is normally worked over one block. To work a complete cross stitch, follow the numbered sequence: bring the

needle up through the fabric at the bottom left corner of the stitch, cross one block of the fabric and insert the needle at the top right corner. Push the needle through and bring it up at the bottom right corner, ready to complete the stitch in the top left corner. To work the adjacent stitch, bring the needle up at the bottom right corner of the first stitch.

To work cross stitches in two journeys, work the first leg of the cross stitch as above but instead of completing the stitch, work the adjacent half stitch and continue on to the end of the row. Complete the crosses by working the other diagonals on the return journey. See also the technique panel page 12.

Cross stitch on evenweave

Cross stitch on evenweave is usually worked over two fabric threads in each direction to even out any oddities in the thickness of the fibres. Bring the needle up to the left of a verti-

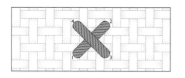

cal thread, which will make it easier to spot counting mistakes. Work your cross stitch in two directions, in a sewing movement, half cross stitch in one direction and then work back and cover those original stitches with the second row. This forms single vertical lines on the back, which are very neat and give you somewhere to finish the raw ends. If you

intend to work over one thread on an evenweave fabric, work each cross individually otherwise the stitches can slip under the fabric threads. See technique panel page 13.

THREE-QUARTER CROSS STITCH

Three-quarter cross stitch is a fractional stitch which produces the illusion of curves when working cross stitch designs. The stitch can be formed on either Aida or evenweave but is more successful on evenweave, as the formation of the cross stitch leaves a vacant hole for the fractional stitch.

1 To work a three-quarter cross stitch, work the first half of the cross stitch as usual, sloping the stitch in the direction shown on the chart you are using. Always work the second 'quarter' stitch over the top and down into the central hole to anchor the first half of the stitch. If using Aida, push the needle through the centre of a block of the fabric. You may prefer to use a sharp needle for this exercise.

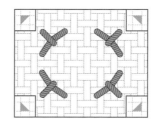

2 Where two three-quarter stitches lie back to back in the space of a full cross stitch, work both of the respective 'quarter' stitches into the central hole.

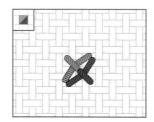

DOUBLE CROSS STITCH

Double cross stitch can be worked over two or four threads of an evenweave fabric or over one or two blocks of Aida, to create a series of bold crosses or 'stars'. Tiny double cross stitches may be formed over two threads of evenweave but they are difficult to work on one block of Aida. To

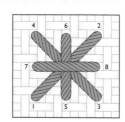

keep all double cross stitches uniform make sure that the direction of the stitches within them is the same.

To work, start to the left of a vertical thread and following the numbered sequence in the diagram, work a diagonal cross stitch and then add a vertical cross on top. The second vertical cross may be worked in a different colour to add interest, in which case work the stitch in two stages – all lower crosses first, followed by the top crosses.

DOUBLE FAGGOT STITCH

This stitch creates textured areas in a design and can be worked as a border or regular pattern for filling in larger areas. The effect created looks particularly good if worked in thread the same colour as the fabric.

1 Bring the thread through the fabric at 1, then insert the needle at 2 (four threads to the right) and bring through at 1 again.

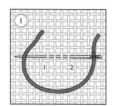

2 Re-insert the needle at 2, then bring it through at 3 (four threads down and four to the left). Stitches must be pulled firmly to achieve the open effect.

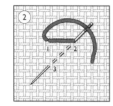

3 Insert the needle at 1 (four threads up) and bring it through at 3 again.

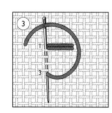

4 Re-insert the needle at 1, then bring it through at 4 (four threads down and four to the left).

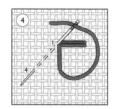

5 Continue in this way, following the number sequence to the end of the row. Complete the last stitch 7–8 by re-inserting the needle in 6 and bringing it out at 8 (four threads down and four to the right).

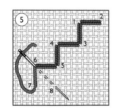

6 Turn the work around to work the last row. Bring the thread through at 8, insert the needle at 7 and bring through at 8 again. Turn the work and repeat the procedure to create four sides to each stitch.

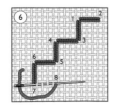

EYELETS

These can be stitched in various shapes and the rules are the same for all eyelets: as with Algerian eye you need to pass the needle down the central hole, working the stitch in the correct sequence and in one direction to ensure that the hole is round and uniform. Take care that trailing threads do not cover the hole as you progress to the next stitch.

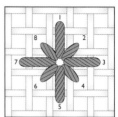

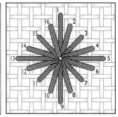

HALF EYELET

This is worked in a similar fashion to a full eyelet but only completing one half.

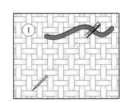

FOUR-SIDED STITCH

Four-sided stitch is traditionally worked as a pulled stitch to create a lacy effect without the removal of fabric threads. It can also be used as a hemstitch when threads are to be cut or removed. The secret of creating a perfect four-sided stitch is to make sure that your needle travels in the correct direction on the back of the stitch. The stitches on the front should be vertical or horizontal but diagonal on the back. It is this tension which forms the small holes as the stitch is worked. The stitch is not recommended for Aida fabric.

1 Begin to the left of a vertical thread and work a horizontal straight stitch across four threads (or the number indicated on the chart), passing the needle *diagonally* across four threads at the back of the work.

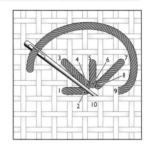

2 Bring the needle up and form a vertical straight stitch, again passing the needle *diagonally* across four threads at the back of the work.

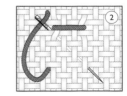

3 Bring the needle up and form another vertical straight stitch, again passing the needle diagonally across four threads at the back.

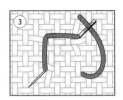

4 Work a horizontal straight stitch to form the last side of the square but this time pass the needle across diagonally to begin the next stitch.

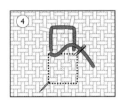

FRENCH KNOT

French knots are small but important stitches though they can cause distress as they are apt to disappear to the back of the work or end up as a row of tiny knots on the thread in the needle! Follow the steps below for perfect knots.

1 Bring the needle through to the front of the fabric and wind the thread around the needle twice. Begin to 'post' the needle partly through to the back, one thread or part of a block away from the entry point. (This will stop the stitch being pulled to the wrong side.)

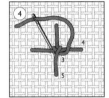

2 Gently pull the thread you have wound so that it sits snugly at the point where the needle enters the fabric. Pull the needle through to the back and you should have a perfect knot in position. If you want bigger knots, add more thread to the needle as this gives a better result than winding more times round the needle.

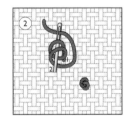

GREEK CROSS STITCH

This pulled stitch looks very ordinary on its own but creates wonderful patterns when worked in groups. The pattern will vary depending on the relative position of each stitch. The stitch needs to be pulled fairly firmly to create the right effect.

1 Bring the needle and thread through at 1, go down at 2 (four threads up and four to the right) then up at 3 (four threads down), keeping the thread under the needle.

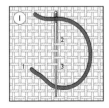

2 Pull the thread through then put the needle down at 4 (four threads to the right) and up at 3 as shown (four threads to left), keeping the thread under the needle.

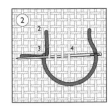

3 Pull the thread through then put the needle down at 5 (four threads down) and up at 3 as shown (four threads up), keeping the thread under the needle.

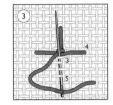

4 Pull the thread through and secure the cross by inserting the needle at 3 to overlap the first and last stitches.

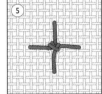

HALF RHODES STITCH WITH BAR

This is an adaptation of Rhodes stitch, producing a decorative stitch shaped rather like a sheat of corn, with a straight bar across the centre to tie the threads together. Buttonhole stitching could be added to the bar.

1 Work over squares of two, four, six or eight threads of evenweave fabric, in a slanting, anticlockwise direction.

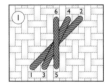

2 Complete the half Rhodes stitch and maintain the same sequence for every stitch to achieve a uniform effect.

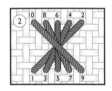

3 To finish, add a single straight stitch across the centre, holding the threads firmly.

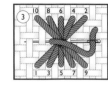

HOLBEIN STITCH

This stitch, also called double running stitch, is the traditional stitch for creating blackwork patterns, which should look the same on the back and front. If backstitch is used instead it creates a rather padded and untidy reverse. (See technique panel on page 67 for further advice on blackwork.) Holbein stitch can be worked in two colours by changing colour before completing the gaps on the return journey.

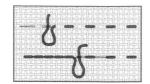

Work a row of running stitch in one direction, counting to ensure that you work under and over two threads of evenweave or one block of Aida, and then work back over the row in the opposite direction, filling in the gaps.

HOLLIE-POINT STITCH

This pretty stitch, also known as holy point, nun's work and point lace, was commonly seen on samplers from the 18th century. The stitch is formed on the front of the fabric and looks like fine knitting.

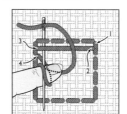

Outline the area to be covered in hollie-point in backstitch with one strand of stranded cotton (floss). Bring the needle out to the front of the fabric and lay a thread across the fabric as in Fig 1. Following the diagrams, work across the laid thread and then repeat across each row.

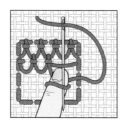

LAZY DAISY STITCH

Lazy daisy is a versatile stitch, particularly useful for flower petals. The stitches formed can be of different lengths and angles as it is not truly a counted stitch. Check the chart for stitch lengths and directions.

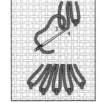

To work lazy daisy, follow the diagram, bringing the needle to the front at 1 and down at 2 forming a loop. Anchor the loop by bringing the needle up at 3 (inside loop) and down at 4 (outside).

LONG-LEGGED CROSS STITCH

Long-legged cross stitch, also known as long-armed Slav stitch and Portuguese stitch, looks wonderful when worked in rows because it forms a plaited-braid effect which is ideal for borders, or for the outside edges of pieces to be made up as a pincushion or a scissor keeper. It can also be worked on Aida across two blocks and upwards over one. The stitch can be used to join sections.

1 To work long-legged cross stitch on evenweave, begin to the left of a vertical thread. Following the numbered sequence, insert the needle four threads forwards and two threads upwards in a long diagonal 'leg'.

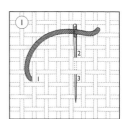

2 Insert the needle two threads upwards and two threads backwards diagonally to make the short leg.

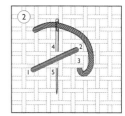

3 To work a row of long-legged cross stitch, follow the numbered sequence shown in this diagram.

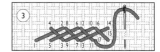

NEEDLELACE

I have used needlelace to create flowers but needlelace is not a modern idea – some 17th century samplers included pretty flower petals created this way. The technique isn't difficult but practising on spare fabric would be helpful.

1 Begin by positioning a glass-headed pin in the material as shown in Fig 1. If using stranded cotton (floss), anchor a pair of threads (or one strand if using perlé cotton) using the loop start method.

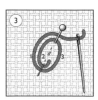

2 Wind the thread around the pin as in Fig 2 and then around again as in Fig 3.

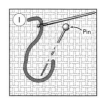

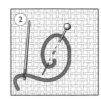

3 When you are at the head of the pin, stop winding and, using the needle, weave in and out of the threads as in Fig 4. It takes a little practice to get an even finish but it is very effective.

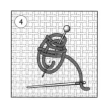

4 When a petal is complete, pass the needle to the wrong side and remove the pin. Repeat the process to make as many petals as you need.

5 When the flower is complete, add some French knots to the centre.

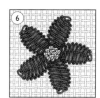

QUEEN STITCH

This stitch is made of four parts and forms little dimples in the embroidery by pulling small holes in the fabric. It is gorgeous when worked as a group. The stitch is traditionally worked from right to left, but if you find this difficult to count, work the two middle parts first followed by the outer ones.

1 Work one long stitch over four threads of the fabric, which is then moved two threads to the right by the needle coming up at 3 and a small stitch worked across one thread.

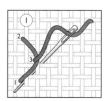

2 Repeat the long stitch from the same position as in Fig 1, but this time bending the stitch over one thread only.

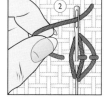

3 Repeat the long stitch from the same position as in Fig 1, but this time the long stitch is bent to the left and the needle re-enters the fabric in the centre position.

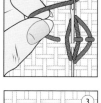

4 The last stage of the stitch is completed forming a lantern shape on the fabric. Note how the top and bottom hole is shared by each stage of the stitch so forming the holes or little dimples that make this stitch distinctive.

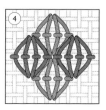

RICE STITCH

Rice stitch is a cross stitch with an additional stitch worked over each 'leg' or corner of the cross. It can be worked in two stages: a row of normal cross stitches, followed by the additional stitches as a second row. This makes it ideal for working in two colours, which

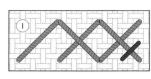

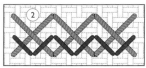

can create very pretty effects. When using two colours, work all large crosses first, followed by the additional stitches in the second colour. Rice stitch is worked over an even number of threads, usually over four threads of an evenweave fabric, but it can also be worked to occupy the space of four blocks of Aida. Do not pull the stitch and form holes around the edge.

To work rice stitch, start to the left of a vertical thread, working a half cross stitch across four evenweave threads, then returning to complete the cross. In the third stage (Fig 2) additional stitches are added in a second colour. These additional stitches across the legs are traditionally worked as a backstitch into each central side hole.

SATIN STITCH

This long, smooth stitch is often used to fill in shapes and can also look very effective when worked in blocks facing in different directions. It can be worked diagonally, horizontally or vertically.

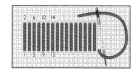

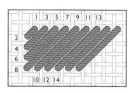

To work satin stitch, start with an away waste knot, which reverses the twist on the thread.

Beginning to the left of a vertical thread, follow the numbered sequence in the diagram, laying flat stitches side by side. Always come up the same side and down the other so that the back of the fabric is covered and the stitches lie closely and neatly beside each other. Take care not to pull too tight (unless working pulled satin stitch – see below).

PULLED SATIN STITCH

Pulled satin stitch is worked in the same way as normal satin stitch but pulling the thread as you stitch forms holes in the fabric and creates a lacy effect.

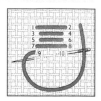

HARDANGER AND FILLING STITCHES

KLOSTER BLOCKS

Hardanger embroidery is a type of counted embroidery distinguished by its cutwork and Kloster blocks form the framework for these cut areas. Start with an away waste knot – you will need to be able to snip off the knot and thread the needle with the away knot thread, so allow enough thread.

1 Kloster blocks are worked in patterns, with 5 vertical or 5 horizontal straight stitches, each of them over 4 threads on evenweave or 4 blocks if on Hardanger fabric. Keep checking that the blocks are directly opposite each other. The vertical and horizontal blocks must meet at the corners and share the same corner hole. If the stitches are worked side by side they will appear on the back of the fabric as shown here. Make sure that you do *not* travel between Kloster blocks at the back unless under existing blocks.

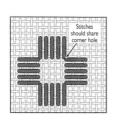

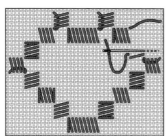

2 When all the blocks are complete and match everywhere, use sharp, pointed scissors to cut across the ends of the blocks. Go slowly, counting and cutting two threads each time. Make sure that you can see both scissor points before cutting.

3 Once the threads are cut, withdraw them, leaving the cutwork area ready for needleweaving, wrapped bars and filling stitches.

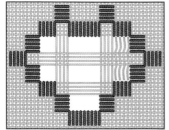

NEEDLEWEAVING

Needleweaving is used to decorate the loose threads that remain when stitched Kloster blocks have been cut. The needleweaving creates covered bars and these bars can be decorated with stitches such as picots, while the spaces between the bars can be filled with decorative stitches such as dove's eye and spider's web.

1 Start by anchoring the thread under adjacent Kloster blocks on the back of the work.

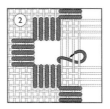

2 Beginning from a cut area, bring the needle up through a void area.

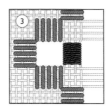

3 Weave the needle under and over pairs of threads to form a plaited effect. The stitches should not distort or bend the threads.

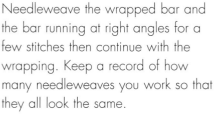

CORNER NEEDLEWEAVING

Corner needleweaving is usually combined with wrapped bars (see below) and can look very effective when used in groups. Use an away waste knot and start by wrapping a pair of threads until you are a few stitches away from an intersection. Needleweave the wrapped bar and the bar running at right angles for a few stitches then continue with the wrapping. Keep a record of how many needleweaves you work so that they all look the same.

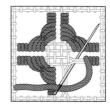

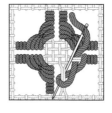

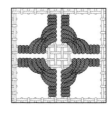

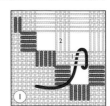

WRAPPED BARS

Like needleweaving, wrapped bars may be worked alone to decorate the threads that remain after cutting or as part of other decorative stitches.

1 Start by anchoring the thread under adjacent Kloster blocks at the back and begin wrapping from a cut area.

2 Wind the thread around and around the four threads, then travel to the next group of threads and repeat. As you wrap each bar hold the threads you are wrapping quite firmly to prevent them unravelling as you work.

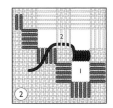

3 Continue wrapping the bars, noting how many times each set is wrapped and keeping the stitches consistent.

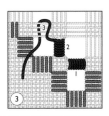

DOVE'S EYE STITCH

This is a traditional Hardanger stitch which is constructed whilst needleweaving.

1 Whilst working the last side of a square, needleweave to the centre of the bar, bring the needle out through a void area.

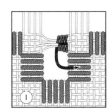

2 Pierce the neighbouring Kloster block or needlewoven bar halfway along its length, bringing the needle up through the void and through the loop formed by the thread.

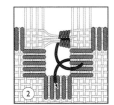

3 Continue around the square following the sequence in the diagram but before resuming the needleweaving, loop the needle under the first stitch to form the final twist in the dove's eye.

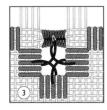

CORNER DOVE'S EYE STITCH

This filling stitch is added in the same way as a dove's eye but is created by working from each corner of the square. Use an away waste knot to start and follow the route taken in the diagram, remembering the last twist to complete the square. Cut off the starting knot and run loose threads into the back of the woven bars.

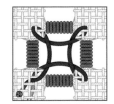

SPIDER'S WEB STITCH

This is a traditional filling stitch used to decorate the voids left by cutting threads and is often used with wrapped bars. Note the number of winds and weaves to ensure stitches are uniform.

1 Work three sides in Kloster blocks, wrapped bars or a combination, bringing the needle out at 1. Cross the square bringing the needle out at 2.

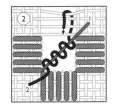

2 Return to position 1, winding the thread around the diagonal just formed, ready to complete the final side, shown as a wrapped bar in Fig 3.

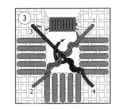

3 Bring the needle up at 3, pass diagonally to 4, then wind the thread around the diagonal to the centre (as in Fig 2).

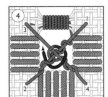

4 Start weaving the spider's web around the diagonals. After three winds you may need to tighten and adjust the position of the winds to ensure that they are even and centred in the square.

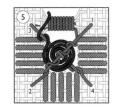

5 When the web is complete, leave the stitch by winding around the diagonal as before.

WOVEN LEAF STITCH

This pretty filling stitch can be worked as a leaf shape on the diagonal or as a fan working from the edge or centre of a needlewoven or wrapped bar. When the framework has been needlewoven, take the thread to the opposite corner and then back to the source. If working across the corner proceed as shown in the diagram.

If working a woven fan take the threads from the centre to the corners and weave as shown.

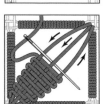

HEMSTITCHING

HEMSTITCH

Hemstitch is wonderfully versatile, allowing you to hem raw edges, form folded hems (see page 20) or remove horizontal threads and decorate the verticals in various ways. When working hemstitches for the first time it is simple to work them without removing threads first, eliminating the anxiety of cutting too many, although traditionally the threads are removed before the hemstitching. When you have perfected the stitch you can experiment with thread removal.

As you can see from the diagrams the stitch is made up of parts, two straight stitches and one diagonal on the back. It is this combination which forms the safe barrier if threads are to be cut or removed. If you are intending to cut to the edge, you may prefer to use double row hemstitch. Hemstitch can look very effective worked in rows without any threads removed. The stitch is not suitable for Aida.

1 This shows hemstitching over two threads in each direction. Work a straight stitch across two threads, turning the needle to face horizontally.

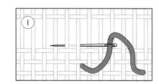

2 Make another straight stitch across two threads, at right angles to the first stitch, then pass the needle down diagonally under two threads.

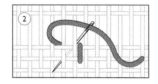

3 Repeat the straight stitches along the row, counting carefully.

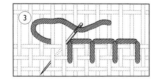

To remove horizontal threads prior to hemstitching, count carefully to the centre of the band and cut horizontal threads (refer to the chart for how many threads). Using a needle, un-pick the linen threads back to the edge of the band. Working in pairs, remove one thread completely and then reweave the other into the gap (see ladder hemstitch diagram, right). Continue until all the threads are removed or rewoven.

DOUBLE ROW HEMSTITCH

To work this version of hemstitch, you first need to withdraw threads either side of a solid fabric area (see chart for how many). As you can see from the diagram the stitch is formed with vertical or horizontal stitches on the front of the

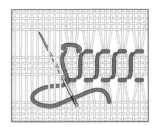

work with diagonal stitches formed on the back. The stitch needs to be pulled quite firmly to create the right effect.

DIAMOND HEMSTITCH

This is an attractive hemstitch variation. Withdraw threads either side of a solid fabric area (see chart for how many) and then work the hemstitch in two journeys. The stitches will form diamond shapes on the front of the work and if pulled firmly will create small holes in the solid fabric area.

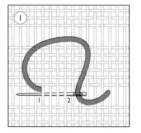

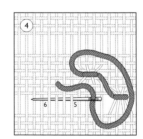

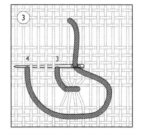

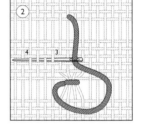

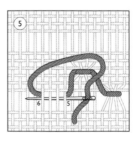

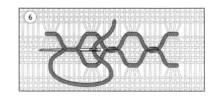

LADDER HEMSTITCH

This is the simplest decorative hemstitch. Cut the horizontal threads (see chart for how many) and reweave them, as shown. Work two rows of hemstitch as described above – the vertical threads that remain form a ladder pattern.

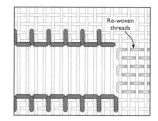

ZIGZAG HEMSTITCH

This is formed in almost the same way as ladder hemstitch. Cut the horizontal threads (see chart for how many) and reweave them, as shown. Work one row of hemstitch as for ladder hemstitch and then work the second row but offset the stitches by one fabric thread to create a zigzag effect.

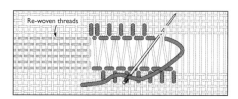

TIED HEMSTITCH

This pretty but very simple hemstitch variation is created by hemstitching two rows, withdrawing the intervening horizontal threads and then using the needle to tie groups of threads together. Begin by stitching two rows of hemstitch as above. Take the needle and thread over a group of four threads (or as chart), knotting them around. The secret of perfection is to ensure that the tying thread is as straight as possible.

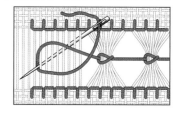

SOMERSAULT STITCH

This stitch is formed on the vertical threads that remain after hemstitching and thread withdrawal.

1 Begin the stitch after thread withdrawal and two rows of hemstitch have been completed. Using the hemstitch thread, bring the needle up at the side centre of the hemstitched frame (you will need to carefully track through the back of the fabric to do this).

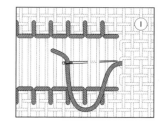

Count four fabric threads and insert the needle under two threads and up between the two pairs, so the needle is positioned over the second pair of threads. Don't pull the needle through the work yet.

2 Without removing the needle from these threads, twist the needle until it faces the other way. The threads will twist automatically as you do this. Pinch your fingers together over this stitch and gently pull the needle through, keeping the thread horizontal and taut. Repeat this process down the row, fastening off into the fabric edge.

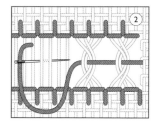

BEADED SOMERSAULT STITCH

This is worked in the same way as somersault stitch above but slipping a bead on in between each stitch.

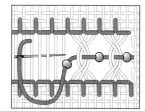

HERRINGBONE STITCH

This simple and decorative stitch (also known as plaited stitch, catch stitch, fishnet stitch and witch stitch), is often used on band samplers, making a fine companion to cross stitch. It looks particularly pretty when combined with stitches like long-legged cross stitch. It can also be whipped with a second colour. It is shown here worked over four evenweave threads diagonally and under two horizontally. It can be worked over two and under one to make it smaller, or over and under more threads to make it larger.

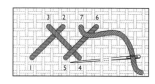

Work the stitch by starting to the left of a vertical thread, across the number of threads indicated on the chart, following the numbered sequence in the diagram.

Finishing and Making Up

*H*ow your embroidery is finished and made up makes a great deal of difference to the look of the piece. This section describes some of the finishing techniques used in the book and shows how the projects were made up.

Washing and Ironing Work

If necessary you can hand wash embroidery. Use bleach-free soap, rinse well and remove excess water by squeezing gently in a soft, clean towel. Dry naturally.

To iron embroidery, cover your ironing board with four layers of towel and steam press the work from the wrong side. Take extra care with buttons, charms and metallic threads.

Stretching and Mounting

Your embroidery will look its best if stretched and mounted. When mounting small cards or novelty projects you can use double-sided adhesive tape, but it is worth taking more time and effort on larger projects.

Most of the framed embroidery in this book has been mounted using polyester wadding (batting) to create a padded finish. The advantage of this is that any slightly lumpy bits on the back of your work will be pushed into the padding rather than appear as raised areas on the front. The padding also raises the embroidery, displaying it to better effect.

To stretch and mount embroidery you will need either acid-free mounting board or lightweight foam board or foamcore.

1 Using a sharp craft knife, cut a piece of foamcore board to fit your frame – an easy way to do this is to cut around the piece of glass that fits the frame.

2 Trim the wadding (batting) to the same size as the foamcore and attach it to the foamcore using double-sided tape. Position your embroidery on top of the padding and centre it carefully on the board. Fix the embroidery in position by pinning through the fabric into the edges of the board. Start in the middle of each side and pin towards the corners, making sure your pins follow a line of Aida holes or a linen

thread so that edges will be really straight. If necessary, adjust the fabric's position until it is centred and straight.

3 Turn the work over, leaving the pins in place, and trim the excess fabric to about 5cm (2in) all round.

There are three methods of attaching needlework to board before framing:
● Pin the work to a covered board and stitch in position.
● Pin the work to the edge of the board and secure with double-sided tape (see diagram, left).
● Pin the work to the board and lace across the back with strong linen thread (see diagram, bottom left).

If pinning your work to a covered board the embroidery must be centred and stretched evenly because any wobbles will show when the design is framed. Measure the board across the bottom edge and mark the centre with a pin. Match this to the centre of the bottom edge of the embroidery and, working outwards from the centre, pin through the fabric following a line of threads until all four sides are complete. You can now either stitch through the needlework to the covered board and lace the excess material across the back or stick it in place with double-sided tape.

Framing

You will see from some of the wonderful photographs in this book, that the way in which a design is framed can greatly affect the end appearance. Mounting and framing by a professional can be expensive, particularly if you want something a little different, but most of the finishing techniques suggested in this book can be tackled by the amateur at home.

Tip

Before fixing in the back board and sealing the frame, line the inside with some aluminium foil which will discourage thunder flies from finding their way in!

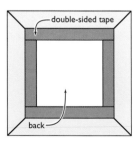

double-sided tape

back

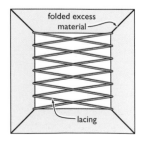

folded excess material

lacing

When choosing a frame for a particular project, select the largest moulding you can afford and don't worry if the colour isn't suitable. Needlework generally looks better framed without glass but if you prefer to use glass you must ensure that the embroidery does not get squashed by the underside of the glass. Either use spacers (narrow strips of board), gold slip or a mount (mat) between the glass and the mounted embroidery to hold them apart. Framed work often benefits from a mount and as you can see from this picture of the Beaded Birth sampler adding a single or double mount (mat) can add dimension to even the simplest projects. Framers have a large selection of mounts in all sizes and colours or will cut one to fit. Ask the framer to make up the frame and a coloured or gold slip for you, but buy the frame, glass and so on in kit form (most framers do not mind!) and then decorate the frame yourself (see Tip).

To frame your stitching, stretch and mount as described opposite and set aside. Place the frame face down on a covered surface and after cleaning both sides of the glass, place the glass in the frame rebate and insert the gold slip, mount or spacer followed by the stitching.

Making Up the Advent Calendar

To make up the Advent Calendar you will need the completed cross-stitched bands, 30.5 x 51cm (12 x 20in) piece of festive cotton fabric, bias binding, decorative ribbons, pineapple bell pull ends and matching sewing thread.

1 Lay the festive fabric on a clean flat surface and lay the cross stitched bands across the width, carefully matching the position of the motifs. Remember to allow enough room to put something in the pockets! Pin and tack (baste) in position.

2 Position the narrow ribbon down the length of the project creating the pockets and reaching the top and bottom of the fabric. Pin, tack (baste) and machine slowly down each side of the ribbon.

3 Make a double fold at the top and bottom of the fabric and machine stitch. This will take in the raw ends of the ribbon and make a channel for the bell pull ends or dowelling rod. To finish, bind the two long sides with bias binding (see below), carefully including the edges of each linen band.

Making Bias Binding

The Rose Case, Sparkly Advent Calendar and Stitcher's Floral Companion are completed using bias binding which can be purchased or home-made.

To make bias binding, cut strips of fabric 4cm (1½in) wide across the grain of the fabric and machine sew them together to make the length needed. To attach bias binding by hand or machine, first cut the binding to the correct length. Pin the binding to the wrong side of the project, matching raw edges and machine or hand stitch. Now fold the binding to the right side and top stitch in position. Press lightly.

Making a Bell Pull

The Sulgrave sampler has been made up into a bell pull, as the other band samplers in this book could be.

Begin by measuring the stitching and allowing your preferred margin and 1.5cm (½in) seam allowance and then select a pair of bell pull ends. The pineapple ends shown in the picture have a wooden rod which can be trimmed to suit the project. You will need: bell pull ends and rod, cotton backing fabric and matching sewing thread.

Cut the backing fabric 2cm (¾in) narrower than the stitched piece. Place the pieces right sides together, pin and machine sew down the two long sides. Turn through to the right side and press from the back, ensuring that the margin on either side of the stitching matches. Folding in the raw ends, fold over the top and bottom narrow edges to form a channel for the bell pull rods. Pin in position and slipstitch invisibly. Slide the rods in position top and bottom and add the bell pull ends. Make a twisted cord from matching threads to hang the bell pull.

Making Cards

There are many blank cards available from needlecraft shops that are simple to use but in this book all the cards are home-made using handmade papers, ribbons and even raffia for the embellishments.

In all cases I cut the design to the required size (allowing for fraying if appropriate) and then selected a coloured card or paper that complemented the thread colours. In some cases I layered coloured papers and even soft felt with great effect. Dolls' house wallpaper and wrapping paper with small all-over designs can also be most attractive.

To attach the embroidery to the card I used double-sided adhesive tape in most cases, adding a dab of craft glue if necessary. Adding ribbon trims is a matter of personal preference and as you can see I like using it!

Making Cushions and Pincushions

Making cushions and pincushions is quite straightforward and the Beaded Bird and Bramble Garland, the Honeysuckle Ring Pillow and the Rose Pincushion can be made up as described here. As you can see by the photographs, the two cushions have been made a little more special by insetting the embroidery into a mitred front (described below).

For a basic cushion or pincushion, place the embroidered piece of fabric and a piece of backing fabric the same size wrong sides together and sew together around all sides, leaving a gap for turning. Turn through to the right side, insert a cushion pad or stuffing and slipstitch the gap closed. The edges can be decorated with twisted cord or braid as desired.

Making a Mitred Cushion Front

A mitred front to a cushion gives it a professional touch and really sets off the embroidery as you can see in the Beaded Bird and Bramble Garland and the Honeysuckle Ring Pillow. Use silk Dupion or moiré to create a sumptuous effect.

1 Measure the embroidery and decide on the size the finished cushion is to be. Allow 1.25cm (½in) seam allowances throughout. Subtract the embroidery measurement from the two finished measurements, divide by two and add on the two seam allowances. This gives the total width of the border pieces. The length of the border pieces is the finished measurement of the cushion cover plus two seam allowances.

2 Press the embroidery face down on several soft towels. Cut the linen to the required size plus two seam allowances.

3 Find the mid-point of each edge by folding and mark with a pin. Fold each border panel in half to find the centre point and mark with a pin. Pin the border panels to the embroidery, matching the centre points and leaving the edges free.

4 Machine stitch these seams around each side of the square. The seams should meet at the corners exactly at right angles. Fold the embroidery in half diagonally, wrong sides together, and mitre the corners by stitching a line from the corner of the embroidery to the corner of the border panels (see diagram). Trim the excess cloth and clip the corners. Repeat for the remaining corners.

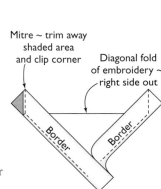

Mitre ~ trim away shaded area and clip corner

Diagonal fold of embroidery ~ right side out

Border

Border

Making Up the Rose Case

The Rose case, Stitcher's Floral Companion and Violet purse were all made up using the basic technique described here. To make up the Rose case you will need: the two completed cross stitch pieces, 45 x 75cm (18 x 29½in) piece of lining fabric, satin bias binding, polyester wadding (batting) and matching sewing thread.

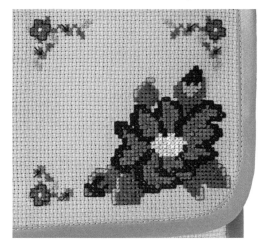

1 If you have used one piece of fabric for the front flap you will need to join this to the remainder of the case. Place right sides together, machine a narrow seam and press open.

To make the rose case up as a patchwork, lay the six pieces of cross stitch face up and arrange as preferred. Trim the fabric pieces so each piece is the same size. Using the seaming method (right sides together, machine a narrow hem, press seam open) join three sections across the width. Repeat with the other three sections and then join the two pieces together, matching corners carefully.

2 Place the patchworked piece on a clean, flat surface and cut a curve to the cross-stitched end of the fabric to make the flap. Make a paper pattern of the shape first if you prefer – the edge of a dinner plate will help you draw curved corners. Cut lining fabric and polyester wadding (batting) to match.

3 Sandwich and pin the cross stitch, wadding (batting) and lining fabric together, right sides out. Machine around the edge and trim away any excess.

4 Using bias binding (see page 117 to make your own), bind the short straight edge that will be the inside of the case. Fold the bound edge up to the middle to form a pocket and tack (baste) in position. Bind up one side all around the flap and down the other side. To attach the bias binding you can either machine first on the wrong side and then top stitch down on the right side, or machine on the right side and slipstitch on the other side if you are nervous about machining a perfectly straight line!

Making Up the Stitcher's Etui
This little case from page 99 is easy to make up. You will need: handkerchief linen or cotton lawn, matching sewing thread and sharp needle.

1 First work a folded hem around the embroidery (see page 20). Lay the hemmed stitching right side down on a clean surface.

2 Cut a piece of handkerchief linen as a lining and fold a narrow hem around it so that it fits just inside the hemstitching. Using a sharp needle, hemstitch the lining in place re-using the holes made when first hemstitching.

3 Fold the bottom section up to the centre, check the position of the embroidery (which will form the front flap), then pin in place. Using matching thread, slipstitch the two sections together to form the pocket.

Making Up the Stitcher's Floral Companion
To make up you will need: the completed cross stitch, 28 x 51cm (11 x 20in) piece of chintz lining fabric, 28 x 51cm (11 x 20in) polyester wadding (batting), satin bias binding and matching sewing thread.

Place the cross stitch on a clean, flat surface, cut a curve to the cross-stitched end of the fabric to make the flap and cut lining fabric and polyester wadding (batting) to match (as described in the Rose case above). Continue to make up following steps 2, 3 and 4 above.

Further Reading

Bishop, E. *A Collection of Beautiful Stitches* (Cross 'N Patch, 2002)

Dillmont, T. *DMC Library: The Encyclopaedia of Needlework* (Bracken, reprinted 1987)

Greenoff, J. *The Cross Stitcher's Bible* (David & Charles, 2000)

McNeill, M. *Pulled Thread Embroidery* (Dover Publications, 1999)

O'Steen, D. *The Proper Stitch* (Symbol of Excellence Publishers Inc, 1994)

The Anchor Book of Counted Embroidery Stitches (David & Charles,1997)

Acknowledgments

It would not be possible for me to work on a book like this without the support of my family - my husband, Bill, and James and Louise. They need a sense of humour, unlimited patience and to enjoy fast food! To my parents, Eric and Pat Fowler who continue to search out my books and magazines and make sure they are on the front of the book stand wherever they are!

My heartfelt thanks to the following: to Sue Hawkins who continues to support me in her work as Technical Director of the Cross Stitch Guild and for her friendship, which even survives working together! To Helen King, whose sense of humour is legendary, and Daphne Cording who has worked so hard for us over the past few months. To Liz Cooke who will do any job you give her with a smile.

Many thanks to my marvellous team of stitchers and pattern testers: Hanne Castello, Lesley Clegg, Sue Moir, Jill Vaughn, Glenys Thorne, Margaret Cornish, Margaret Pallant, Susan Bridgens, Deborah Buglass, Liz Burford, Jacqueline Davies, Doreen Ely, Elizabeth Edwards, Jean Fox, Joyce Halliday, Joan Hastewell, Rikki How, Gina How, Janet Jarvis, Amanda Lake, Margaret Locke, Su Maddocks, Sue Smith and Suzanne Spencer.

Thanks to all the generous suppliers of the materials and equipment required for this book: Rainer Steiman of Zweigart for lovely fabrics, DMC Creative World and Coats Crafts UK for stranded cottons and metallic threads and Ian Lawson Smith for his wonderful I.L.Soft computer programme. And to all the other suppliers who supplied anything I asked for whilst writing this book.

Grateful thanks also to the Trustees of Sulgrave Manor, Sulgrave, near Banbury, Oxon OX17 2SD. Tel: +44 (0) 1295 760205. www.sulgravemanor.org.uk

Thanks to Cheryl Brown at David & Charles for continuing to have faith in me and Linda Clements for her tireless work checking yet another manuscript! A special thank you to Ethan Danielson for all the excellent technical stitch diagrams and beautiful charts that make this book so special. Thanks to the Country Flower Company, Bishops Walk, Cirencester 0800970 1080 for the lovely flowers in the photographs and to Simon Whitmore and Ali Myer for the scrummy photographs.

Suppliers

UK Suppliers
If ringing from outside UK use +44, no (0)

Burford Needlecraft
117 High St, Burford OX18 4RG, UK
Tel: +44 (0) 1993-822136
For general needlework supplies, including Caron threads (also mail order)

The Button Box
PO Box 289, London WC2E 9SG, UK
Tel: +44 (0) 207 240 2716
For wooden buttons (butterfly and bird house)

The Country Cross Stitcher
19 Bedford Street, Woburn, Bedfordshire MK17 9QB, UK
Tel: +44 (0) 1525 290070
Fax: + 44 (0) 1525 290072
Website: www.countrycrossstitcher.co.uk
For general needlework and quilting supplies, including Caron threads and Au Ver à Soie

The Cross Stitch Guild
Yells Yard, Cirencester Road, Fairford, Gloucestershire GL7 4BS, UK
Tel: +44 (0) 1285 713799
Website: www.thecrossstitchguild.com
For a wide range of needlework supplies, including cross stitch fabrics, linen bands, bell pull ends, buttons, charms (including bees and butterflies) & gold-plated needles

Terata Ltd
Unit 8, Heath Business Centre, Heath Road, Hounslow, Middlesex TW3 2NF, UK
Tel: +44 (0) 20 8230 3080
Website: www.terata.co.uk
For decorative buttons

The Paper Shed
March House, Tollerton, York YO61 1QQ, UK
Tel: +44 (0) 1347 838253
Fax: +44 (0) 1347 838096
Email: papershed@papershed.com
Website: www.papershed.com
For decorative papers, including dolls' house wallpapers

Crafty Ribbons
3 Beechwood, Clump Farm, Tin Pot Lane, Blandford, Dorset DT11 7TD, UK
Tel: +44 (0) 1258 455889
Website: www.craftyribbons.com
For decorative ribbons

Francis Iles
73 High St, Rochester ME1 1LX, UK
Tel: +44 (0) 1634-843082
For general needlework supplies, including Caron threads and Au Ver à Soie threads

Pearsall's Embroidery Silk
Tancred Street, Taunton, Somerset TA1 1RY, UK
Tel: +44 (0) 1823 274 700
Fax: +44 (0) 823 336824
info@pearsallsembroidery.com

DMC Creative World Ltd
Pullman Road, Wigston, Leicestershire LE18 2DY, UK
Tel: +44 (0) 116 281 1040
Fax: +44 (0) 116 281 3592
Website: www.dmc.com
For a full range of needlework supplies, including threads and Zweigart fabrics

Coats Crafts UK
PO Box 22, Lingfield, McMullen Road, Darlington, County Durham, DL1 1YQ, UK
Tel: +44 (0) 1325 365457 (for stockists)
Fax: +44 (0) 1325 338822
For a wide range of needlework supplies, including Anchor threads

US Suppliers

Caron International Yarns
US contact: Ed Hamrick
Caron PO Box 222, Washington, NC 27889, USA
Tel: 800 868 9190
Fax: 252 975 7309
Website: www.hamrick@caron.com
For Caron threads

Kreinik Manufacturing Co Inc
3106 Timanus Lane, Suite 101, Baltimore, Maryland 21244, USA
Tel: 1 800 537 2166 or
1 410 281 0040
Fax: 1 410 281 0987
Website: www.kreinik.com
For Kreinik metallic and silk threads

M & J Buttons
1000 Sixth Avenue, New York, NY 10018, USA
Tel: 212 391 6200
Website: mjtrim.com
For ribbons, buttons, beads and trimmings

Yarn Tree Designs
PO Box 724, Ames, Iowa 500100724 USA
Tel: 1 800 247 3952
Website: www.yarntree.com
For cross stitch supplies and card mounts

Zweigart/Joan Toggit Ltd
262 Old Brunswick Road, Suite E, Picataway, NJ 08854-3756, USA
Tel: 732 562 8888
Website: www.zweigart.com
For cross stitch fabrics and linens

Index

Page numbers in **bold** type refer to main entries.